"I want to leave it distinctly on record that no one need have died of famine in Ireland. For a fraction of the cost of the Kaffir War, we can be spared the shame of letting our fellow citizens die."
Edward Twisleton.

Portrait of Edward Twisleton, Commissioner for Poor Laws in Ireland, 1845-1849. Twisleton was in charge of the administration of the workhouses in Ireland during the worst years of the famine. He resigned in protest at the policies of the Prime Minister, Lord John Russell.
Portrait reproduced with kind permission of the Hon. Martin Fiennes.

To Jan

Copyright Dymphna Mayne Headen
Published by Crom Cruaich Publications 2018
ISBN number 978-0-9930488-1-4

www.notthepotato.com

2

"LITTLE JACK HORNER."

LITTLE JACK HORNER
Sat in a corner,
Eating his Parliament Pie;

He put in his thumb
And pulled out *his* Plum,
And said, "What a good Boy am I!"

Lord John Russell was Prime Minister during the Irish Famine. This carton from Punch in 1847 shows him with a bag of money to help the starving Irish. He gave only a quarter of this to Ireland.

Image courtesy of the National Library of Ireland

Contents

Introduction

It is generally accepted that the reason for the Great Irish Famine of 1845-1850 was that the potato crop failed and therefore the people starved. I offer you a different explanation for the famine. The potato did not cause the Great Hunger in Ireland. It was the building of the workhouses, and the taxes raised to pay for them, which caused the calamity.

161 workhouses were built in Ireland, between 1840 and 1853. The building started in 1840, five years before the famine. Universal taxation was introduced in Ireland, for the first time, to pay for the building of these workhouses. When the people could not pay, they were evicted, and they went to the workhouses. The taxes were increased to pay for the extra people, and the country was bankrupted by these taxes.

Workhouses were first introduced in England in 1834. 600 workhouses were built there between 1834 and 1850. They were huge buildings, constructed like prisons, which could house 1,000 people at a time. They were the only places where people could go, who were homeless and starving. They were, in fact, prisons for the poor.

Everybody knows about Victorian workhouses from the writings of Charles Dickens. When Oliver Twist asked "Please Sir, can I have some more gruel?" we get an insight into how the poor were treated in Victorian England. Workhouses may have been a good idea in England for owners of factories. The idea of the workhouse frightened the people and put pressure on them to work in factories and mills rather than go into a workhouse. Ireland however was an agricultural country and the people did not have the option of working in a factory. For that reason the building of workhouses, and the tax imposed on the people to pay for them, sent the country into ruin.

I believe that my suggestion can be proved by examining the debates in Parliament during that period. These records are now easily accessible on the internet for anyone to check. I believe these records show that the conditions which created the famine had more to do with government policy than with the potato. It is also important that these records are contemporaneous with the events that led up to the famine, and so the judgements are those of the politicians of the period.

It was misleading of the Government to call the famine "The Potato Famine". It should have been called "The Poor Law Famine", because of the policies of the government which introduced the Poor Laws for Ireland.

Yes, there was a potato blight in Ireland in the winter of 1845-46. But it was not the potato blight which caused the famine. It was the Poor Laws and the building of the workhouses. At the time Isaac Butt said 'The poor laws will make all Ireland poor.' He was right.

The Poor Laws for Ireland

There was absolutely no need for workhouses to be built in Ireland in the 1840's. The people of Ireland were much too poor to pay for a massive building program. Yet the aristocrats in the government in London insisted that Ireland needed workhouses. The person who was responsible for the building of the workhouses in Ireland was Lord John Russell. Lord Russell was Home Secretary from 1835 to 1839, and was Prime Minister from 1846 to 1852, during the worst years of the famine.

When Russell was Home Secretary in 1837, he introduced a Bill in Parliament "For the more effectual Relief of the destitute Poor in Ireland". This name was misleading. It was a Bill which did not protect the poor in any way. It set out the framework for building 161 workhouses in Ireland. This led to a building boom in Ireland, and this then led to austerity when the people were taxed in order to pay for these buildings.

Workhouses were presented to the English middle classes as a solution to the problem of vagrancy. The rising middle classes of Victorian England were bothered by the masses of beggars and thieves on the streets, as so vividly portrayed by Charles Dickens. Anti vagrancy laws were passed with the object of getting rid of the vagrants on the streets. They could be locked up in workhouses to stop them begging. This cleaning up of the streets was a justification for asking for taxes from the middle classes.

However that was in England. In Ireland there were no factories and no middle classes and workhouses were not suited to the country. Daniel O'Connell said "you might as well build a wall around Ireland and call it the workhouse".

The first 131 workhouses in Ireland were built in a space of three years, between 1840 and 1843. A second lot of 30 workhouses were built between 1849 and 1853.

The cost of the first 131 workhouses was £1,200,000. This would be billions of pounds in today's money. As soon as they were built, Lord Russell established an administration to tax the people of Ireland to pay for them.

Lord Russell was one of the political elite. He was the fourth son of the Duke of Bedford. He was descended from King Charles II through the King's relationship with Louise de Kerouaille. Russell had a reputation for being clever and devious.

King William IV called Russell "a dangerous little radical". In 1834 Russell was put forward as Leader of the Whig party in the House of Commons. The King opposed the appointment. The King showed good judgement. Irish politicians may have had reason to agree with King William in the years which followed.

In 1836 Russell sent one of the English Poor Law Commissioners to Ireland, to report on whether a system of workhouses could be set up there, similar to that which had been established in England two years earlier. The English Poor Law Commissioner who came to Ireland was George Nicholls. He spent only six weeks in Ireland and came back with a lengthy report and a Bill already prepared to go to Parliament. It would seem that his visit was just a pretext for the introduction of this Bill. It was probably written by Nassau Senior, who had been an advisor on the English Poor Laws. The Bill set out that Ireland would be divided into Unions, that each Union would have a Workhouse, and that each Union would hold elections to appoint a Board of Guardians to run the Workhouses.

The elections were confined to the landlord class. At that time in Ireland, the population was 8 million people, but only 67,136 had a vote. Voting was open only to those who held land of £8 valuation or higher. Very few of the population of Ireland had land of any value.

This landlord class was to be responsible for the management of the workhouses when they were built. They were given power, status and authority, but they did not receive a salary for these duties. To be appointed a Guardian was to be given a poisoned chalice, as it created tensions between Guardian landlords and their tenants. It was the responsibility of the Guardians to make sure that the rates were collected from the tenants. This led to the eviction and starvation of a large number of the population of Ireland. It also created the conditions which led to a number of landlords being murdered, such as Major Mahon in Strokestown Co Roscommon, who was a member of the board of guardians of the Roscommon workhouse. He had chartered a ship for his tenants to emigrate to Canada. Many tenants died on the way. On his return from a meeting of the guardians of Roscommon workhouse he was shot dead.

In his speeches in parliament Russell consistently blamed the potato for what happened to the Irish during the famine. That innocent vegetable was only a symbol which distracted attention from the unfair laws which were imposed on the Irish people. The potato was not the problem, and yet to this day the failure of the potato crop has become the accepted explanation for the famine that we know as the Great Hunger.

George Nicholls the administrator

The person who was in charge of the administration of the Poor Laws was George Nicholls. He was a Poor Law Commissioner for England at the time he was appointed. Nicholls was a man with a colourful history. He was apprenticed as a sea going officer at the age of sixteen on a ship owned by the East India Company. By the age of 34 he had become a captain of another East India ship, the Bengal. It was burnt in a harbour in Ceylon and he had to pay for the loss of the ship. He resigned from the East India Company, and went on to become manager of a bank in Birmingham. He also became an administrator of a Parish Workhouse in Southwell. While he was there, he reduced the diet of the paupers in the workhouse, and made conditions more severe. As a result, he cut the cost of running the workhouse for the Board of Guardians. This brought him to the attention of Lord Russell, who appointed him as one of three commissioners of the English Poor Law Board. Clearly, Russell liked the qualities which Nicholls displayed of frugality and miserliness. Nicholls had all the attributes of Dickens' character Scrooge, from "A Christmas Carol".

In later years Nicholls was involved in a scandal about the manner in which English paupers were treated. There was a workhouse in Andover, in Hampshire, where the paupers were put to work crushing bones of horses, dogs, and cattle, for bone meal fertilizer. The paupers were so hungry that they sucked the marrow from the bones. This created a scandal, and there was a House of Commons inquiry, in 1846. As a result, the jobs of Nicholls and the other two Commissioners were abolished. Nicholls however survived the scandal. A new Poor Law Board was set up in its place. He was assigned as permanent secretary to this Board. The loyal employees of the Establishment were always protected and rewarded.

In 1836 Nicholls was already the trusted administrator of Lord Russell. When Russell sent him to Ireland to report on whether to build workhouses there or not, he knew that he would get the right answer. There would be no misunderstandings and no surprises. On 22 August 1836, Russell wrote a letter to Nicholls setting out what were to be the terms of his inquiry in Ireland. In it he said "there is no one to whom I can entrust such a duty, more able to perform it with judgement and diligence than yourself".[1] In this letter it is very clearly spelled out exactly what Russell expected Nicholls to recommend. He was to report on two things. The first was on how to set up a 'machinery' or administrative system to collect rates, and administer workhouses, and the second was whether some provision could be made to encourage the population to emigrate. On the first Russell directed Nicholls to inquire if a system of setting up Unions and appointing Guardians to collect rates would be feasible. He wrote "You will carefully weigh the important question-whether a rate… might be usefully directed to the erection and maintenance of workhouses…".

What Russell expected was some system of collecting rates from the people. Russell wrote "You will specially direct your attention to the machinery by which any rates for the relief of the poor might be raised and expended".

This was a major undertaking, which would require a large body of staff to implement. It would introduce a tax on the majority of the Irish people for the first time.

The second objective contained in the instructions of Lord Russell to Nicholls was that of emigration. He was asked to report on the possibility of setting up centres where emigrants could stay before they embarked for the British Colonies. The idea of promoting emigration was always part of Russell's plan for the poor of Ireland. The Boards of Guardians were given the option of paying for people to stay in the workhouse or paying a once off sum for them to emigrate. After 1848 more emphasis was laid on this, and large sums of money were paid to paupers to emigrate, particularly from the most distressed areas in the south and west.

The recommendations of George Nicholls had already been decided before he ever came to Ireland. Nevertheless, he duly reported back that 100 workhouses should be built there. He estimated that the cost of building these 100 workhouses would be £700,000. As expected, he proposed that the cost of the workhouses should be raised by imposing a tax on the Irish population. The loan would be spread out over twenty years. For the first ten years no interest would be charged. No figure was given as to the amount of interest which would have to be paid for the following ten years, when the workhouses would be up and running, Nicholls said that the extra cost of the food and administration of the workhouses would be £295,000 a year. This amount would be added to the annual repayment of the workhouse loan. In total, Nicholls stated this would cost the people of Ireland £345,000 annually to pay for the building of the workhouses and their upkeep. In the end, of course, the cost of building the workhouses soared, and the cost of maintaining paupers in the workhouses rose to an alarming extent.

There had been a previous commission set up by Parliament, in 1834, to inquire into what steps could be taken to assist Ireland's poor. This commission had been headed by Archbishop Whateley, the Protestant Archbishop of Dublin. It had made several reports, in one of which it was said that workhouses were not suited to Ireland, and should not be built there. Lord Russell ignored those reports. He wrote in his letter to Nicholls "Your attention need not be very specially given to the

[1] George Nicholls, *Three Reports to her Majesty's Principal Secretary of State*. HMSO, London 1838
This letter is reproduced in the Appendices.

plans for the general improvement of Ireland, contained in the report of the Commissioners of Inquiry".

The Bill "for the more effectual Relief of the Destitute Poor in Ireland" became law in 1837, and in 1838 George Nicholls was sent to Ireland as Poor Law Commissioner. He set up his office in Dublin Castle, and brought a large staff of English civil servants with him. They divided Ireland into 131 Unions and made plans to build 131 workhouses. It was in fact the introduction of a system of local government for Ireland. There would be a workhouse in the centre of every Union, and the collection of rates would be organised from each workhouse. There would be elected Boards of Guardians in each local area, who would be supervised by Inspectors from the Poor Law Commissioners' Office in Dublin Castle. All of this was done under the pretence of helping the destitute poor in Ireland. It was actually a measure to control the poor and to manipulate them. It was a scheme of social reorganisation on a massive scale, which led to disaster for Ireland. As the M.P. for Roscommon, Fitzstephen French, said in the House of Commons in later years, the Poor Law "swept away half the gentry, and almost depopulated the entire country". [2]

The Irish opposition to the Poor Laws

When Lord Russell introduced the Poor Law Bill in Parliament, the Irish members were totally opposed to it. Daniel O'Connell made an eloquent speech, on 28 April 1837 pointing out that the plan to build 100 workhouses in Ireland, to house 80,000 poor people, was totally the wrong plan to deal with the poverty there. He drew attention to the report of the Whateley Commission, which said that 585,000 Irish people owned no land, and were out of work for seven months of the year. If all these people were to be given shelter in a workhouse, there should be 4000 workhouses in Ireland, and yet the country could not afford to pay for 100 workhouses. The landlord class would be bankrupted in order to pay for these buildings.

O'Connell criticised George Nicholls for insisting that assistance would only be given to the poor if they entered a workhouse, as in England this was not the case. In England it was the practice to give outdoor relief to the poor. The law in Ireland was to be much more harsh than in England. O'Connell asked the government to spend money giving employment to the poor, rather than in building all these workhouses. His speech makes stirring reading. In his speech he recounted the past history of British injustice in Ireland. He referred to the Penal Laws which prohibited the Irish Catholic population from receiving an education. The Penal Laws also laid down that the Irish could be imprisoned for sending a child abroad to be educated. In fact it was an uncle of Daniel O'Connell, known as the smuggler, who took that risk and sent him to be educated in France. The Penal Laws also prohibited the Irish Catholic from owning land or even owning a horse with a value of more than five pounds.

Daniel O'Connell was an eloquent speaker and a most resourceful barrister. He was the first Catholic to be elected as a Member of Parliament after the passing of the Catholic Emancipation Act in 1829. O'Connell then campaigned for a Repeal of the Act of Union of 1800. He was committed to achieving this through peaceful means. His method was to hold Monster meetings in places which were important in Irish history. One of these was held in Tara in 1843. It was attended by a million

[2] House of Commons Debate, *Poor Rates (Ireland)*, 26 March 1849.

people. O'Connell then planned to hold another monster meeting in Clontarf, near Dublin. This was partly intended as a tribute to William Smith O'Brien, the Member of Parliament for Limerick. O'Brien's ancestor, Brian Boru, was killed in 1014, at a battle against the Vikings, in Clontarf. When O'Connell announced that he would hold a monster meeting in Clontarf, Sir Robert Peel brought gun boats into Dublin Bay and threatened to fire into the crowds if O Connell continued with the meeting. O'Connell cancelled it. Peel had him arrested anyway and held in prison. This sentence was for a year in prison, but the House of Lords reduced it to three months on appeal. O'Connell was so affected by the attitude of Peel towards him that he agreed to support Lord Russell and his party. It would seem he went from the frying pan into the fire.

William Smith O'Brien was another key figure and powerful voice in Parliament in the struggle against the Workhouse project and the Poor Law. In contrast to O'Connell, William Smith O'Brien belonged to the Protestant ascendency. He was educated in the public school, Harrow, in England, and afterwards at Cambridge University, where he was President of the Cambridge Students' Union. His home was Dromoland Castle, the grand stately home in Co Clare. He could have been included in the inner circle of MP's in London if he so wished. Smith O Brien served as an MP for twenty years and in that time he became very critical of the policies of England in Ireland. He was very opposed to the building of the Workhouses in Ireland, and to the Poor Laws. He said that

> it gave unlimited power to three gentlemen in Somerset House. (That is the three Poor Law Commissioners). They would have the power to build 10,000 workhouse, or 10. They could levy a rate of 20 shillings in the pound (100%) or one halfpenny in the pound. I would not confer powers so undefined and unlimited upon any body of men, even if they were perfect as angels, still less would I bestow them upon a board, which, in the administration of the English Poor-laws—whether the system they pursue be bad or good, I will not pronounce— have contrived to excite throughout England a very great amount of discontent and dissatisfaction—but, least of all, would I establish such an uncontrolled despotism in Ireland... If they wished, they could destroy the whole of the property of Ireland to pay for these workhouses, and they would not have helped the poor in any way.[3]

Another powerful voice raised in opposition to the workhouses was that of Isaac Butt, Professor of Political Economy, in Trinity College, Dublin. He wrote a pamphlet of 40 pages to the then Lord Lieutenant of Ireland, Lord Morpeth, asking him to use his influence to stop this Poor Law[4]. He said "in truth it will prove to be a law which will live up to its name, for it will make all of Ireland poor".

He continued:- if Lord Morpeth thought about the condition of the poor in Ireland "You never would have put forward, as a remedy, a measure so entirely- if the subject were not so fearfully solemn;-I would add, a measure so ludicrously inadequate and irrelevant as the workhouses of Mr. Nicholls".

Lord Morpeth was Chief Secretary for Ireland from 1835 to 1841. He came from an illustrious family, the family of the Duke of Devonshire. His grandmother Georgina Cavendish, the Duchess of Devonshire, was a famous beauty, who had a relationship with Earl Grey, and there was a scandal as

---

[3] House of Commons Debate, *Poor Law (Ireland)*, 28 April 1837.

[4] Isaac Butt, *The Poor Law Bill for Ireland examined, in a letter to Lord Viscount Morpeth, M.P. His Majesty's Principal Secretary of State for Ireland.* London. 1837.

a result. Georgina Cavendish was separated from her children and banished from her home.[5] Earl Grey went on to have an illustrious career as Prime Minister of England, but Georgina Cavendish was banished to live in France. In the Victorian world, women were regarded as second class citizens. The blame attached to the woman, and the man was held in high regard.

Lord Morpeth was presented with an illuminated address when he left Ireland in 1841. It was signed by the most distinguished citizens of Ireland. It was so long, that it had to be held in the form of a roll. It was known as Lord Morpeth's rolls. It is now held in the Royal Irish Academy in Dublin. In Lord Russell's letter to Nicholls of 1836 Russell stated that Lord Morpeth would render him every assistance in his power while he was in Ireland. The letter of Isaac Butt fell on deaf ears.

A group in the House of Lords also entered a statement dissenting from the Poor Law Bill, in a debate on 9 July 1838. They said that Irish society was already showing signs of unrest, and that it would be better to restore peace and tranquility before attempting to build workhouses for the poor. They wrote "A measure more impolitic and fraught with mischief never was divised".

They stated that this Poor Law would never be effective in giving support to the poor. The Lords who signed it were Carbury, Mount Cashell, Hawarden, Teynham, Glengall, and Clonbrock.

In spite of all the objections, Lord Russell continued with his plan to establish workhouses and levy rates in Ireland.

The theories of Malthus influenced Lord Russell

There were a number of influential theories around at the time which may have influenced Lord Russell in his plans to set up workhouses in Ireland. The most important of these were the theories of the Rev. Thomas Malthus (1766 to 1834). Malthus wrote that the world population was growing too fast, and there would not be enough food to feed all these extra people. The result would be that people would die through famine, or through war.

In his book "On Human Happiness and World Population, (An essay on the Principle of Population)"[6], Malthus showed that the world population was doubling every forty years. The food which the world was producing was not increasing at this rate. Malthus recommended that the best solution to this problem was for men and women not to have children until they knew that they could provide for them. If they were careless about this, it was inevitable that famines would occur. It was almost inescapable. He wrote that there were 'positive and preventative checks to the growth of the population'. What he called 'positive checks' were famine and war. 'Preventative checks' were control of the birth rate, and postponement of marriage. Famine and war were inevitable if the population grew too fast. If Lord Russell subscribed to this thinking, he might well have thought that if a famine occurred in Ireland, it was just the inevitable effect of too fast a growth in the population. More than likely he was happy to use it as an excuse, when there was famine in Ireland.

---

[5] In the film "The Duchess", Kiera Knightly played the role of Georgina Cavendish, and Ralph Fiennes played the character of the Duke of Devonshire. Ralph Fiennes is of the family of Lord Saye and Sele and would be a distant relation of Edward Twisleton, the Poor Law Commissioner for Ireland.

[6] Malthus, *An Essay on the Principle of Population; or a view of its past and present effects on Human Happiness.* London 1806. (First edition published anonymously 1798, London.)

The economic theories of Malthus were exceedingly influential, particularly on the policies of the East India Company. He held the position of Professor of Political Economy at the East India Company College, Haileybury, in Hertfordshire. The East India Company was one of the most powerful commercial institutions of the United Kingdom at that time. It controlled trade between India, China and the United Kingdom. Undoubtedly it influenced the policies of the U.K. Government and was a major player behind the scenes.

When the Company set up a school in Haileybury in England to prepare young men for the Indian Civil Service, it was taken for granted that these young men would also form part of the administration of Ireland. Many of the names which are familiar to us in Ireland were of men who had also been employed by the East India Company in India. Charles Trevelyan served in India for fourteen years. He became the Under Secretary of the Treasury from 1841 to 1852. It was he who was the chief administrator of government policies in Ireland during the famine. George Nicholls, the Poor Law Commissioner, had been captain of a ship belonging to the East India Company. Sir William Gregory, who introduced the Gregory clause in the Irish Poor Law Extension Act (1847), became Governor of Ceylon. Cornwallis, who spent seven years as Governor-General of India, was the man who came to Ireland in 1798 to organise the Act of Union between England and Ireland. This Union came into effect on 1 January 1801.

The opinions of Malthus were taken very seriously by the Government of the time. In 1827 there was a House of Commons Inquiry into the possibility of using emigration to improve the lot of the English Poor. Malthus was called as an expert witness to the Inquiry. He spoke in favour of emigration as a safety valve for population growth. He was particularly insistent that it would be important that Irish labourers should be assisted to emigrate. The report stated

> he was satisfied that no permanent improvement would take place in the case of the English poor, if a portion of them were removed by emigration, as long as this influx of Irish labourers into England continued without a check. Mr. Malthus stated, that unless a change took place in the management of land in Ireland, he can only anticipate an increase in poverty and misery: and that such change cannot take place, unless something is done to remove the people.

He was asked his thoughts on evictions, and his reply was, that if Irish Labourers were to be evicted, it would be necessary to pull down the houses immediately afterwards. Otherwise the peasant would return to the house when the evictors were gone. He said

> If the landlords in Ireland were making a change in the management of their estates and were altering the distribution of their land, I think it is possible that the vacuum might not be filled up, because those miserable hovels that had been deserted might be pulled down and not be replaced. [7]

Malthus died in 1834, but his opinions were influential for many years to come. When Irish tenants were evicted during the famine, the practice of pulling down their houses was followed. His

_____

[7] Parliamentary Papers. 1826-27 (550), *Third Report from the Select Committee on Emigration from the United Kingdom.* 1827. Page 312 of 665.

opinions about restricting the growth of population were also influential. It was the rule in workhouses that men and women were to be segregated, which had the effect of ensuring that the population did not increase. (although there were exceptions).

Malthus wrote that farmers should have a reasonable size of a farm in order to be comfortable. This thinking was also expressed by Lord Russell in 1849, when he put forward a proposal to help English settlers to buy farms in Ireland, from which people had been evicted. Russell said then that Englishmen might be persuaded to come over who had capital to spend on the farms and who could develop larger farms. As it happened, very few English farmers took up the offer of cheap farms in Ireland. They said they could not predict how high the rates would finally go. Also the labourers who would work the land had all died or emigrated.

The ideas of Malthus not only had a great influence on the administrators who ruled India and Ireland in the 19th century but they also gave a veneer of respectability to the Poor Laws passed by the government in England in the 1830's and 1840's.

England had a previous experience of creating a famine when it imposed too much taxation on a population. This happened in Bengal in 1770, when ten million people died. The blame was attributed to a drought in 1769 and the failure of the rice crop, but many historians blamed the high taxes. In 1865 the East India Company had defeated the Moghul ruler of Bengal, and in the treaty of Allahabad the East India company secured the right to raise taxes. By 1770 they had increased the taxes from 10% to 50% and there was a famine. Amartya Sen, a Nobel Prize winner, and economist, described it as a man made famine. He pointed out that there had been no famine in Bengal in the previous century, and he showed that many famines occur even when there is an abundance of food. In his book "Entitlements and Deprivation", he illustrated the fact that in many cases famine is a result of political action, rather than a lack of food.[8]

Ireland and India both were administered as colonies of England. Malthus was a lecturer in Political Science in the East India Company School in Hailebury. His ideas would have been influential on the future administrators of the Empire. These ideas would form some of the approach of the government in London during the Irish Famine.

---

[8]Amartya Sen, *Poverty and Famines*, Oxford University Press, 1961.

Building and Financing of the Workhouses

Griffith's Poor Law Valuation

Maps serve many purposes. In Ireland the maps served as an instrument to collect taxes. In 1826 the Government directed that the Army in Ireland would draw up maps for the Ordnance Survey. The man appointed to carry out this survey was Richard Griffith. Griffith worked out of Dublin Castle, where he had a staff of army personnel, who drew up maps of Ireland. He also employed Irish speakers to record the Irish names of townlands, and to translate them into English. These Ordnance Survey maps were the maps which the Boards of Guardians used when the workhouses were set up. The Guardians had to decide on the rate which all the land owners and tenants in their union must pay. Different Boards of Guardians charged different rates. There was a demand for a uniform rate throughout all of Ireland. The Government decided to set up a new Valuation Office in 1846 and Richard Griffith was appointed as the Valuation Commissioner.

Griffith had a distinguished career as a geologist. He had discovered deposits of coal in Arigna in Co. Leitrim, and in other places around Ireland. He worked as a geologist for the Royal Dublin Society for years. He had published many books on the geology of Ireland, and frequently gave lectures on the subject. He was awarded the Wollaston Medal for geology in 1853. This medal was a prestigious award. It was awarded to Charles Darwin in 1859.

The survey which Griffith undertook in the Valuation Office became known as "Griffith's Poor Law Valuation". It took until 1857 to complete. In 1858 Griffith was knighted for his work in the Valuation Office.

His survey gave the names of all the occupiers of land in Ireland. The amount of rates which each person must pay was based on "Griffith's Poor Law Valuation". Most people do not stop to consider the name of this valuation. Even today every house in Ireland is valued according to Griffith's Poor Law valuation. It is called the "Poor Law" valuation, because it was a system designed to collect taxes to pay for the Workhouses which were set up under the Poor Laws. It has become a most valuable resource for the descendants of Irish emigrants who wish to find out where their ancestors came from. It is an irony that it is the record which caused their ancestors to pay rates for the first time, and which was the means by which many Irish people were evicted from their farms, which is the resource of such importance today. Without it, and without the Poor Laws, these descendants might still be living in their ancestral homes.

Sir Richard Griffith was part of the larger administration which organised Ireland into different districts which they called Unions, or Poor Law Unions. Each of these Unions was to have a workhouse in the centre. Each workhouse had an office for the clerk. It was the duty of the clerk to store maps, and to keep the records of the tax collections. It was the duty of the Guardians of the workhouses to appoint tax collectors, and to strike a rate for the sum which was to be collected in their Union. The Guardians became responsible to the Poor Law Commissioners in Dublin, for the amount of rates which were to be collected. The Workhouse was in effect the local County Council Office. It was the work carried out by Richard Griffith which laid the foundation for the imposition of the new taxes. Without these maps, no tax could have been levied on property in Ireland.

George Wilkinson - Architect.

The architect appointed to design all the workhouses in Ireland was just 25 years of age when he came to Ireland. He was George Wilkinson (1814 to 1890), from Oxfordshire. He created only two designs. One was for the first 131 workhouses, which were built between 1840 and 1843, and one for thirty workhouses which were built in the second phase, between 1849 and 1853.

Wilkinson made one valuable recommendation to George Nicholls and Lord Russell. He recommended that no beds should be provided in workhouses. Instead he proposed that the dormitories would have a sleeping platform five inches high. Sacks filled with straw could be put on this platform, for the paupers to sleep on. This would mean a considerable saving, and this appealed to George Nicholls.

The workhouses were very austere. They were built on the model of prisons. Daniel O'Connell referred to them as "Bastilles for the Poor." Families were split up the moment they entered the workhouse. Women were sent to one side of the buildings and men to the other. Children over the age of two were put in a separate building away from their parents. Each compound was separated from the next by high walls. Families would see each other just once a week, at Mass. The influence of Malthus can be seen in this policy. True to Malthus' principles here would be no opportunity for parents to have more children.

Russell believed that conditions in a workhouse should be so harsh that no poor man would think of entering one unless he was destitute. He saw this as an incentive to the population to work hard or to emigrate. He called it the "workhouse test." This "workhouse test" was effective in England, where there were factories to provide the people with employment. In Ireland this was not the case. The only work available was agricultural work, and this was seasonal.

Not only were the workhouses built on the model of a prison, solitary confinement cells were also in the plans, to enforce discipline. These were called "refractory cells", for paupers who were disobedient, or "refractory". They were single stone cells, with a stone ceiling which had vents for air in it, and a stone bed. Paupers could be locked up in these cells for days.

Wilkinson designed the workhouses, but he did not personally oversee the erection of the buildings. This was done by Assistant Commissioners. Eleven Assistant Commissioners were employed in the Poor Law Commissioners Office in Dublin Castle. Each had a large district to supervise. These officers were in constant touch with Boards of Guardians, and could overrule them. They made the important decisions. These included which contractor would get the contract to build the workhouse. The guardians had no authority to make this decision. In England, individual Boards of Guardians could appoint their own architect. Many of the English workhouses were designed by famous architects such as George Gilbert Scott or Sampson Kempthorne. This was not the case in Ireland.

There was widespread dissatisfaction with the way in which the workhouses were built. William Smith O'Brien criticised Wilkinson in a speech in the House of Commons in 1843:-

> They have expended above 1,200,000l. This large sum has been laid out under directions of an architect who was brought over from England, and who appears to have been wholly unacquainted with the prices of work in Ireland, and to have been in other respects very incompetent. About the taste of his designs, it is not necessary to raise a question. The order

of architecture is a sort of spurious Elizabethian. In the opinion of those who are most capable of forming a judgment, it is considered a very expensive style of building; and it is obvious to everyone conversant with the details of such institutions, that, for the purposes of internal arrangement, a less eligible plan could scarcely have been devised. It is impossible in these buildings, to adopt a proper classification of the inmates; and, if infection is once introduced, it can scarcely fail to spread through the whole establishment.[9]

The Poor Law Commissioners continued with their work unconcerned with these criticisms. In 1844 Wilkinson gave a justification for the problems with the workhouse buildings in an Appendix to the Pennethorne report. He had to defend his building plans and the very high payments which he authorised, and his competence was questioned in Parliament by William Smith O'Brien and many others.

In 1845 Wilkinson published a book called "The Practical Geology and Ancient Architecture of Ireland". This was surely an attempt to enhance his reputation. It is a book which has much information on the geology of Ireland and it clearly owes more to the scholarship of Sir Richard Griffith than to the research of Wilkinson himself. Griffith had published many books on the geology of Ireland and he was then Assistant Commissioner of the Board of Works in Dublin. He may have been ready to assist Wilkinson, who would not have had the time to undertake such a project. Most of the drawings in the book were not done by Wilkinson himself, they were done by assistants in his office. His book has all of the appearance of an attempt to bolster up his reputation on the part of the Poor Law Commissioners.

Wilkinson remained in Ireland until 1888, and was responsible for the design of many railway stations, including Harcourt Street station in Dublin. His designs for the Irish workhouses gave expression to the policies of Lord Russell for the poor of Ireland. The workhouses were grim, punitive, enclosing, and a source of terror for the Irish population. This was the vision of Lord Russell for the poor.

William Smith O'Brien and Pennethorne's Inquiry into the workhouse buildings

There were frequent references in Parliamentary debates to the fact that the staff of the Poor Law Commissioners were rude and overbearing. The Assistant Commissioners were mainly English and they did not know the conditions of the country they were in. Fitzstephen French complained about "the arbitrary and offensive manner in which commissioners dealt with the poor-law guardians, endeavouring to reduce them to mere ciphers, the utter ignorance of the condition, habits, and feelings of the Irish people they had shown, the contemptuous disregard for considerations of the highest importance they had displayed...[10]

William Smith O'Brien was one of the main critics of the Workhouse system in Ireland. He took over the role of main spokesman for Ireland in 1843, when Daniel O Connell was sent to prison by Prime Minister Peel.

William Smith O'Brien asked in the House of Commons for a copy of all the correspondence of the Poor Law Commissioners in relation to the construction of the Irish Workhouses. It is thanks to

---

[9] House of Commons Debate, *Poor Law (Ireland)*, 23 March 1843.

[10] House of Commons Debate, *Poor Law (Ireland)*, 05 May 1843.

him that we have so much information on the supervision and construction of the workhouses, and of the complaints of the Boards of Guardians. The main complaints were about the dampness of the buildings. It appeared that no mortar was used to plaster the walls on the outside. There were insufficient water supplies, and there was no thought given to where the effluent from the latrines would go. There were also complaints about the way the windows were put in. In an effort to save on putty, the windows were put in dry, and the rain poured in from the outside. When there were a large number of people in the dormitories the moisture produced was high, and the air was damp. The chances of infection spreading were increased. Wilkinson had made a feature of how the bed platform would be ventilated, with pipes for air running underneath it, but it still was not efficient.

There was also a problem with the floors. Wilkinson had stated that clay floors would be sufficient for the inmates in the areas which they were to occupy. This was a considerable saving. He wrote that it was what the Irish peasant was used to. These floors were made of clay and mixed with ox blood. In one report the Guardians complained that the smell from the decomposing ox blood was highly offensive. The Poor Law Commissioners ordered that the inmates should take up the floor and lay it again.

Shortly after Smith O Brien received the report of the Poor Law Commissioners, and probably because of his enquiries, the government ordered an independent enquiry into the construction of the workhouses in Ireland. The man entrusted with the enquiry was James Pennethorne. He was an eminent architect, and a student of the architect John Nash, who built Regent's Park in London. He came to Ireland and visited 63 workhouses without telling the Poor Law Commissioners that he would be inspecting their work. Pennethorne reported that there had been widespread negligence in the building of the workhouses. In the conclusions to his report, Pennethorne said that the workhouses were not always sound and substantial, and very seldom staunch. He wrote

> Although it cannot be said that the Boards have been wilfully deceived, they have been greatly misled, because they were each fully justified in their expectation that for the sum borrowed they would have had a sound, substantial, and stanch house, in lieu of which the houses are not always sound and substantial, and very seldom stanch; they have been declared in many instances fit for the reception of paupers, in an unfinished state, with imperfect drainage, without a sufficient supply of water, without boundary walls or ditches to enclose the ground, and, in some instances, almost without any proper approach to the entrance door; they have cost more than the Commissioners virtually undertook to build them for; and many Boards have had to incur out of the rates of the Union heavy additional expences to complete them. [11]

The Tory Government was sensitive to the criticisms in the Pennethorne report. They sent it to George Nicholls and to Wilkinson to ask them for their comments, before they published it. The excuses of Wilkinson and Nicholls were added as an appendix to the report. This was an unusual approach for the government to take. George Nicholls said that he would never have gone to Ireland if he had known that he would be subjected to scrutiny of this sort.

---

[11] Parliamentary Papers 1844, *Report of Commission for inquiring into the Execution of the contracts for certain union workhouses in Ireland* (562) (568). Vol. XXX 387, 551.

The Duke of Wellington criticised the report in the House of Lords. He said the Government wished to have a second opinion on the findings of Pennethorne. The government sent over Lieutenant-Colonel Barney of the Royal Engineers to conduct another inquiry. Not surprisingly Barney found that the workhouses had all been very well built. He did say that there had been some small imperfections. He recommended that 12½% be deducted from the cost of the workhouses. Otherwise, he said they were buildings "fully worth the money the Guardians will be required to pay." [12]

The Government accepted the recommendations of Lieutenant Colonel Barney of the Royal Engineers. Without the vigilance of William Smith O'Brien, we would not know that there were so many shortcomings in the building of the workhouses in Ireland.

---

[12] Parliamentary Papers 1845 (170), *Union Workhouses (Ireland).Copy of report of the Commissioner appointed to inquire into the Execution of the Contracts for certain Union Workhouses in Ireland*, &c. Vol. XXVI 399.

Collecting the new taxes

The workhouse buildings were completed in 1843, at which stage the government then started to collect the rates to pay for these workhouses. The people resisted paying this money, and there were riots throughout the country. The government then employed the army to accompany the rate collectors. The army had the power to seize animals and crops, if the people did not pay.

In March 1843 Fitzstephen French asked in the House of Commons if it were true that a large crowd had protested in Waterford against the collection of rates? He said

> he wished to be informed whether the report was correct, that 4000 armed men had entered Waterford, from a neighbouring barony, and had taken possession of the city, stating their determination to resist the collection of poor-rates, under the recent law? He regretted also to have to put another question to the noble Lord, founded upon a statement he had seen to-day in the newspapers, that a collector of poor-rates had been found with his brains beaten out by stones, but the amount of poor-rates he had collected untouched in his pocket? [13]

The Lord Chancellor said that he had no knowledge of this. Yet he was obviously aware that there was going to be a problem with collecting small amounts of money from hundreds of small tenants. Fitzstephen French then requested a return to the House of Commons of "the dates and places where Military or Police have been employed in enforcing the collection of rates, between January 1843 and January 1844".

The information given in the return to the House of Commons showed that a Troop of Cavalry, or a Company of Infantry, were often sent out with a rate collector to collect the rates.[14] In Skibbereen it was stated that "A spirit of Resistance to the payment of the Poor Rates is evinced by the Peasantry" and a troop of Cavalry was positioned in Skibbereen to enforce the Levy of the Poor Rate. Skibbereen went on to become one of the places in the country to suffer most from the famine.[15]

There were very many cases in which 100 militia and ten constables had gone to towns and villages to protect the rate collector, and had got very little money. One example was that of the town of Ballymote in Sligo, where 78 military men were employed on 5 December 1843 and where only 1 pound 5 shillings and 6 pence was collected.

The Government decided to take another course. The Chief Secretary for Ireland, Lord Eliot (3rd Earl St. Germans), pointed out how difficult it was to collect rates from tenants with very little money or land. In Parliament he said

> He held in his hand a return of such cases in different places in Ireland. In Monaghan, for instance, there was an old woman's case, in which the valuation was 15s.; the rate she was called upon to pay was 3½ d. She was unable to pay, and a distress being put on her house she gave an old shawl to get rid of it. There was the case of a man named Snell; the valuation

---

[13] House of Commons Debate, *Poor-Laws (Ireland)*, 20 March 1843.

[14] Parliamentary Papers.1844(186)(218), Poor Relief Ireland(Ireland) Act. *Further return of the Dates on which and the Places where the Military and Police have been employed in enforcing collection of the Poor Rates in Ireland.* Page image 2 of 16.

[15] Parliamentary Papers. 1843 (275), *Poor relief (Ireland). Return relative to erection of poor houses, education of paupers, salaries of officers, expenditure and rates.* Page image 152 of 152.

was 15s, the rate 3½d. There were six in his family, and they all went out to beg for the amount. Another man was rated at the same amount, 3½.d. He was supported only by charity, and having been confined to his bed for a long period was unable to pay the rate. He could multiply such instances almost to infinity, but the consequence was the collection of the rate in such instances became almost impossible.[16]

What he suggested was that people who held land of under £4 in valuation would not have to pay the rate themselves, but that the landlord or the person who leased the land to them, the lessor, would have to pay

> It was open to the Government to take one of two courses—either, as they proposed, to rate the lessor instead of the occupier, or to entitle the occupier to deduct the rate from the lessor. It might appear immaterial, at first sight, which of these courses was adopted, but he believed that, by adopting the former plan, the difficulty of collecting the rate, to which he had already alluded, would be in a great measure obviated.

The Government then passed an Act "for the further amendment of an Act for the more effectual relief of the Destitute Poor in Ireland" in 1843, making a law that lessors had to pay the rates for those with land under £4 in valuation. This pressure did not exist in previous famines. It was this law which made matters much worse during the famine. When the poor tenant could not pay, the landlord became responsible for very large sums of money for all the people on his land. It then became a choice for him whether to pay the money himself and go bankrupt, or to evict his tenants and therefore have no extra rates to pay.

20

---

[16] House of Commons Debate, *Poor Law (Ireland)*. 5 May 1843

Evictions

There are many distressing pictures of Irish peasants and Irish villages shown in books about the famine. Villages stand derelict. The people are gaunt, dressed in rags, with bare feet and a look of hopelessness about them. What is not said about these pictures is that most of these sketches are of people who have been evicted. The houses in the villages have been tumbled. They have no roofs, they give no shelter. This is the awful truth about the famine, many people were thrown out of their houses and left to die in ditches during that time. The Irish M.P. John Reynolds quoted statistics on evictions in the House of Commons in 1849. He said:-"in the three years from Hilary Term 1846, to Hilary Term 1849, both inclusive, the following ejectments took place

	No. of Actions of Ejectments.	No. of Persons Evicted.
1846	4,671	19,864
1847	10,857	51,233
1848	16,385	68,456
1849 (the first quarter)	4,707	19,771

These figures show that during that time 160,000 persons were evicted from their homes.[17]

These statistics are of legal evictions, where the landlord or his agent went to court to get agreement to evict tenants. There are many accounts of hundreds being cleared off the land with no legal authority whatsoever. It is difficult to give figures for the numbers who were evicted without a "habere" permission, but it is likely to be at least double the amount of the legally evicted. As an indication of the number who were evicted without any legal sanction, Captain Kennedy, Poor Law Inspector in the Union of County Clare, gave a figure of 20,000 people who were evicted in Kilrush, out of a population of 80,000 people. These figures would suggest that at least half a million people were evicted during the years of the famine.

One reason for these evictions was that it was part of a movement towards "land clearance", to enable the landlords to change from tillage to pasture. It was clear that there was a demand in England to repeal the Corn Laws, and that cheap wheat and cereals from America would soon be flooding into England. It would no longer be profitable for land owners to cultivate these crops. If a landlord were to make a profit on his land, he would have to raise sheep or cattle. He would no longer require labourers as tenants on his land.

There had been evictions before the famine, but the numbers were small. Evictions increased dramatically from 1845 to 1850. It was convenient to blame the potato blight for the mass clearances which took place, but there was actually a deliberate policy to change the structure of land ownership in Ireland during that time. The workhouses formed a part of this policy. The landlord could say that there was now a place where evicted people could go. An article in the Illustrated London News of 1849 said that

---

[17] House of Commons Debate, *The Kilrush Evictions*. 08 June 1849.

As long as there was no legal provision for the poor, a landlord had some repugnance to drive them from every shelter; but the instant the law took them under its protection, and forced the landowner to pay a rate to provide for them, repugnance ceased: they had a legal home, however inefficient, to go to; and eviction began.

The first notorious mass clearance which took place during the famine and which was reported to the House of Commons was that of a Mrs. Gerard, in Galway, in 1846. William Smith O'Brien read a copy of a report from the Freeman's Journal of 25 March 1846 into the record of the House of Commons. The report described how the houses were demolished and the people had nowhere to go. Many of them slept in the ditches, and quite a few died.[18]

There were many other cases of evictions reported in the House of Commons. One particularly harsh one was that carried out by a Mr. Blake, in Galway, on New Year's Eve 1847. The case was reported to the Irish Poor Law Commissioners by the Temporary Poor Law Inspector, Major M'Kie.[19] He said that

it was an act of great cruelty. Many of those ejected from their houses died of the cold in the wintry days which followed.[20]

The issue of evictions was raised many times in the House of Commons, and the government was asked to intervene. The government of Lord Russell replied that legally, a landlord had a right to evict his tenant, as long as he gave notice. The Attorney General said

If a landlord gave a notice to quit to a tenant, after the period of his tenancy had expired, such landlord had a perfect right to enter the premises, provided he did so peaceably.[21]

Another case of a mass eviction was that of a Mr. St. George, the M.P. for Galway, in March 1847. These evictions were in the islands of Lettermore and Garumna in Co. Galway.[22]

The number of evictions increased dramatically when it became known that Lord Russell was going to introduce a new Poor Law, in 1847. This law was the Poor Law Extension Act. The law provided that every able bodied person who was destitute would be entitled to relief. Before this, only those who were sick and old people and children were entitled to relief. Under the new law, landlords would have to pay a much increased rate to give outdoor relief and to increase accommodation in the workhouse for able bodied paupers. This motivated more landlords to evict their tenants.

There were many cases of evictions reported in Parliament, and in local newspapers. The Anglo Celt published a list of the number of people who had been evicted in the year ending in April 1848. The list gave the names of landlords including Colonel Vandeleur, the Marquis of Angelsey,

---

[18] House of Commons Debate. 2 April 1846. Ejection of Tenantry, Ireland.

[19] Major McKie died of the fever in 1848. This was mentioned in the First Report of the Poor law Commissioners in 1848.

[20] House of Commons Debate, *Forcible Ejectments (Ireland)*. 24 March 1848.

[21] Ibid.

[22] House of Commons Debate, *The case of Mr. St. George*. 04 April 1848.

T.B.Balfour, Lord Ventry, the Earl of Glengall, Lord V. Southwood, R. Gore, the Earl of Lucan, the Earl of Bessborough (the Lord Lieutenant), Lord Oranmore, and R. D. Browne Esq. M.P., who all evicted their tenants. The list is reproduced in the appendix.

In 1848 the House of Commons passed a bill stating that 48 hours notice must be given to the clerk of the workhouse, or the relieving officer of the workhouse, before a family would be evicted. The reason for this was that the workhouse would then be prepared to receive the family. The provisions of the Bill were largely ignored. The government did pass a bill in 1848 that from then on, no one could be evicted one hour before sunset, or two hours after sunrise, and especially, no one should be evicted on Christmas day or on Good Friday, as these were the days of the Lord. The Bill was called "A bill for the Protection and Relief of the Destitute Poor Evicted from their Dwellings in Ireland."

This did not ease the predicament of those poor tenants who were evicted. Two of the more notorious evictions reported to Parliament in 1849 were the evictions of Toomevara, and the evictions in Kilrush. These were reported by Captain Kennedy, the temporary poor law Inspector for County Clare. He raised his concerns about these evictions. He said

> I would not presume to meddle with the rights of property, nor yet to argue the expediency or necessity of these "monster clearances"; both one or the other no doubt frequently exist; this however renders the efficient and systematic administration of the Poor Law no less difficult and embarrassing.[23]

Captain Kennedy sent a list to the Poor Law Commissioners with details of the families who were evicted. The account included heart rending comments, such as

> I, not long since, found a widow woman whose three children were in fever, occupying the piggery of their former cabin, which lay beside them in ruins; …her piggery was knocked down as soon her children were able to crawl out on recovery: and she has now gone forth a wanderer.

The M.P for Stroude, Poulett Scrope, went to Ireland to see for himself the devastation which was caused by these evictions. He toured County Clare with Captain Kennedy. Poulett Scrope wrote an account of the scenes he saw. Wherever he went in the Union of County Clare he saw traces of evictions, and of the work of "the levellers":-

> I passed continually the traces of the 'levellers'. Sometimes eight or ten broken gables of stone-built houses were seen to rear their blackened and skeleton frames against the sky, betokening what had once been a comfortable hamlet - now a pile of ruins.[24]

---

[23] Parliamentary Papers, *Reports and returns relating to evictions in the Kilrush Union.* 1849 (177)
A page of this report is reproduced in the Appendices.
[24] George Poulet Scrope, *Some notes of a tour of England, Scotland and Ireland, made with a view to the inquiry whether our labouring population be really redundant.* London 1849.

Poulett Scrope was a formidable advocate for Ireland. He was often the first to raise questions about the unjust treatment of the Irish, in the House of Commons. He was an eminent geologist, who won the Wollaston medal for his work on volcanoes. He warned that there would be a revolution in Ireland similar to the one in France if the government did not change the way Ireland was being administered. He said

> You are sitting placidly in Downing-street on the apex of a volcano. Frozen snow about you—your heads in the clouds. But far beneath, at the foundation of the social superstructure of Ireland, is a mass of molten fire, boiling, swelling, and bursting for an issue. If you delay long, be sure you will witness an awful explosion, such as will uproot society in Ireland from its base, and leave in its place an abyss of unfathomable horror.[25]

The volcano he foresaw did not erupt. The people continued to be evicted.

[25] House of Commons Debate, *Protection to life (Ireland),-Adjourned Debate-* (Third Night). 06 April 1846.

MISS KENNEDY DISTRIBUTING CLOTHING AT KILRUSH.

CONDITION OF IRELAND.
ILLUSTRATIONS OF THE NEW POOR-LAW.

(Continued from page 394.)

HAVING last week introduced this important subject to our readers, and given them some of the statistics of Kilrush, we shall henceforward allow our Correspondent to speak for himself:—

I assure you (he says) that the objects of which I send you Sketches are not sought after—I do not go out of my way to find them : and other travellers who have gone in the same direction, such as Lord Adair, the Earl of Surrey, and Mr. Horsman, will vouch, I am sure, for the accuracy of my delineations. The Sketch of Moveen, to which I now call your attention, is that of another ruined village in the Union of Kilrush. It is a specimen of the dilapidation I beheld all around. There is nothing but devastation, while the soil is of the finest description, capable of yielding as much as any land in the empire. Here, at Tullig, and other places, the ruthless destroyer, as if he delighted in seeing the monuments of his skill, has left the walls of the houses standing, while he has unroofed them and taken away all shelter from the people. They look like the tombs of a departed race, rather than the recent abodes of a yet living people, and I felt actually relieved at seeing one or two half-clad spectres gliding about, as an evidence that I was not in the land of the dead. You may inquire, perhaps, and I

am sure your readers will wish to know, why it is that the people have of late been turned out of their houses in such great numbers, and their houses just at this time pulled down, and I will give you my explanation of this fact.

The public records, my own eyes, a piercing wail of woe throughout the land—all testify to the vast extent of the evictions at the present time. Sixteen thousand and odd persons unhoused in the Union of Kilrush before the month of June in the present year ; seventy-one thousand one hundred and thirty holdings done away in Ireland, and nearly as many houses destroyed, in 1848 ; two hundred and fifty-four thousand holdings of more than one acre and less than five acres, put an end to between 1841 and 1848 : six-tenths, in fact, of the lowest class of tenantry driven from their now roofless or annihilated cabins and houses, makes up the general description of that desolation of which Tullig and Moveen are examples. The ruin is great and complete. The blow that effected it was irresistible. It came in the guise of charity and benevolence ; it assumed the character of the last and best friend of the peasantry, and it has struck them to the heart. They are prostrate and helpless. The once troublesome people—even the saucy beggars—have disappeared, and given place to wan and haggard objects, who are so resigned to their doom, that they no longer expect relief. One beholds only shrunken frames scarcely covered with flesh—crawling skeletons, who appear to have risen from their graves, and are ready to return frightened to that abode. They have little other covering than that nature has bestowed on the human body—a poor protection against inclement weather ; and, now that the only hard from which they expected help is turned against them, even hope is departed, and they are filled with despair. Than the present Earl of Carlisle there is not a more humane nor a kinder-hearted nobleman in the kingdom ; he is of high honour and unsullied reputation ; yet the Poor-law he was mainly the means of establishing for Ireland, with the best intentions, has been one of the

chief causes of the people being at this time turned out of their homes, and forced to burrow in holes, and share, till they are discovered, the ditches and the bogs with otters and snipes.

BRIDGET O'DONEL AND CHILDREN.

The instant the Poor-law was passed, and property was made responsible for poverty, the whole of the landowners, who had before been careless about the people, and often allowed them to plant themselves on untenanted spots, or divide their tenancies—delighted to get the promise of a little additional rent—immediately became deeply interested in preventing that, and in keeping down the number of the people. Before they had rates to pay, they cared nothing for them ; but the law and their self-interest made them care, and made them extirpators. Nothing less than some general desire like that of cupidity falling in with an enactment, and justified by a theory—nothing less than a passion which works silently in all, and safely under the sanction of a law—could have effected such wide-spread destruction. Even humanity was enlisted by the Poor-law on the side of extirpation. As long as there was no legal provision for the poor, a landlord had some repugnance to drive them from every shelter ; but the instant the law took them under its protection, and forced the landowner to pay a rate to provide for them, repugnance ceased : they had a legal home, however inefficient, to go to ; and eviction began. Even the growth of toleration seems to have worked to the same end. Till the Catholics were emancipated, they were all—rich and poor, priests and peasants—united by a common bond ; and Protestant landlords beginning evictions on a great scale, would have roused against them the whole Catholic nation. It would have been taken up as a religious question, as well as a question of the poor, prior to 1829. Subsequent to that time—with a Whig Administration, with all offices open to Catholics—no religious feelings could mingle with the matter : eviction became a pure question of interest ; and while the priests look now, perhaps, as much to the Government as to their flocks for support, Catholic landlords are not behind Protestant landlords in clearing their estates. English notions and English habits, without any reference to the causes of English

SCALPEEN OF TIM DOWNS, AT DUNMORE.

The Illustrated London News put the blame for the destitution in Ireland on the New Poor Laws of Lord Russell.

MISS KENNEDY DISTRIBUTING CLOTHING AT KILRUSH.

CONDITION OF IRELAND.
ILLUSTRATIONS OF THE NEW POOR-LAW.

(Continued from page 394.)

HAVING last week introduced this important subject to our readers, and given them some of the statistics of Kilrush, we shall henceforward allow our Correspondent to speak for himself:—

I assure you (he says) that the objects of which I send you Sketches are not sought after—I do not go out of my way to find them ; and other travellers who have gone in the same direction, such as Lord Adair, the Earl of Surrey, and Mr. Horsman, will vouch, I am sure, for the accuracy of my delineations. The Sketch of Moveen, to which I now call your attention, is that of another ruined village in the Union of Kilrush. It is a specimen of the dilapidation I behold all around. There is nothing but devastation, while the soil is of the finest description, capable of yielding as much as any land in the empire. Here, at Tullig, and other places, the ruthless destroyer, as if he delighted in seeing the monuments of his skill, has left the walls of the houses standing, while he has unroofed them and taken away all shelter from the people. They look like the tombs of a departed race, rather than the recent abodes of a yet living people, and I felt actually relieved at seeing one or two half-clad spectres gliding about, as an evidence that I was not in the land of the dead. You may inquire, perhaps, and I

am sure your readers will wish to know, why it is that the people have of la been turned out of their houses in such great numbers, and their houses just this time pulled down, and I will give you my explanation of this fact.

The public records, my own eyes, a piercing wail of woe throughout the land all testify to the vast extent of the evictions at the present time. Sixtee thousand and odd persons unhoused in the Union of Kilrush before t month of June in the present year; seventy-one thousand one hundred as thirty holdings done away in Ireland, and nearly as many houses destroyed, 1848 ; two hundred and fifty-four thousand holdings of more than one acre a less than five acres, put an end to between 1841 and 1848 : six-tenths, in fact, the lowest class of tenantry driven from their now roofless or annihilated cabi and houses, makes up the general description of that desolation of which Tullig a Moveen are examples. The ruin is great and complete. The blow that effect it was irresistible. It came in the guise of charity and benevolence; it assum the character of the last and best friend of the peasantry, and it has struck the to the heart. They are prostrate and helpless. The once frolicsome people even the saucy beggars—have disappeared, and given place to wan and hagga objects, who are so resigned to their doom, that they no longer expect relief. O beholds only shrunken frames scarcely covered with flesh—crawling skeletons, w appear to have risen from their graves, and are ready to return frightened to th abode. They have little other covering than that nature has bestowed on the hum body—a poor protection against inclement weather ; and, now that the on hand from which they expected help is turned against them, even hope is d parted, and they are filled with despair. Than the present Earl of Carlisle the is not a more humane nor a kinder-hearted nobleman in the kingdom; he is high honour and unsullied reputation; yet the Poor-law he was mainly t means of establishing for Ireland, with the best intentions, has been one of t

chief causes of the people being at this time turned out of their homes, and forced to burrow in holes, and share, till they are discovered, the ditches and the bogs with otters and snipes.

The young daughter of Captain Kennedy, the Poor Law Inspector, gave away her clothes to the poor.
Image courtesy of the National Library of Ireland.

BRIDGET O'DONNEL AND CHILDREN.

The instant the Poor-law was passed, and property was made responsible for poverty, the whole of the landowners, who had before been careless about the people, and often allowed them to plant themselves on untenanted spots, or divide their tenancies—delighted to get the promise of a little additional rent—immediately became deeply interested in preventing that, and in keeping down the number of the people. Before they had rates to pay, they cared nothing for them; but the law and their self-interest made them care, and made them extirpators. Nothing less than some general desire like that of cupidity falling in with an enactment, and justified by a theory—nothing less than a passion which works silently in all, and safely under the sanction of a law—could have effected such wide-spread destruction. Even humanity was enlisted by the Poor-law on the side of extirpation. As long as there was no legal provision for the poor, a landlord had some repugnance to drive them from every shelter; but the instant the law took them under its protection, and forced the landowner to pay a rate to provide for them, repugnance ceased: they had a legal home, however inefficient, to go to; and eviction began. Even the growth of toleration seems to have worked to the same end. Till the Catholics were emancipated, they were all—rich and poor, priests and peasants—united by a common bond; and Protestant landlords beginning evictions on a great scale, would have roused against them the whole Catholic nation. It would have been taken up as a religious question, as well as a question of the poor, prior to 1829. Subsequent to that time—with a Whig Administration, with all offices open to Catholics—no religious feelings could mingle with the matter: eviction became a pure question of interest; and while the priests look now, perhaps, as much to the Government as to their flocks for support, Catholic landlords are not behind Protestant landlords in clearing their estates. English notions and English habits, without any reference to the causes of English

This is a popular image of the famine. It is not often mentioned that Bridget O Donnell was evicted.

This scene from the Illustrated London News 1849 shows Bridget O'Donnell of Garraunnatooha, Kilmacduane Parish, Kilrush, Co. Clare. She was evicted when she was seven months pregnant. She said:-"I was carried into a cabin, and lay there for eight days, when I had the creature (the child) born dead. I lay for three weeks after that. The whole of my family got the fever, and one boy thirteen years old died with want and with hunger while we were lying sick."

The Illustrated London News says it was easier for Landlords to evict their tenants once the workhouses were built.

Image courtesy of the National Library of Ireland.

VILLAGE OF MOVEEN.

greatness—which are not to be found in a Poor-law and farms of a particular size—impressed law-makers and the landlords of Ireland with a strong desire to enlarge and consolidate farms, and clear them of the squatters and sub-tenants, who had formerly been permitted, if not encouraged. With a Poor-law, that desire could be safely acted on, and so it supplies a temptation and the means to carry eviction extensively into effect.

by the chilliness and dreariness of a November evening, and by the wet and mire in which the naked feet of the crowd were im-mersed. On Captain Kennedy being appointed to the Union, his daughter was much affected by the misery of the poor children she saw; and so com-pletely did it occupy her thoughts, that, with the consent of her parents, she gave up her time and her own little means to relieve them. She gave away her own clothes—she was allowed to bestow part of her mother's—and she then purchased coarse materials, and made up clothing for children of her own age; she was encouraged by her father and some philanthropic strangers, from whom she re-ceived sums of money, and whose example will no doubt be followed by those who possess property in the neighbourhood; and she devoted herself with all the energy and perseverance of a mature and staid matron to the holy office she has undertaken. The Sketch will, I hope, immortalize the beneficent child, who is filling the place of a saint, and performing the duties of a patriot.

On all sides I hear praises of the amiable child and her excellent father, and this is not without a moral for the landlords. The public officers who are ap-pointed to administer and control the relief of the poor, have it in their power to do much for the people. Mere kindness of manner, though they render no substantial assistance, endears them to the suffering crowd. Captain Kennedy is at once kind, charitable, and judicious. He is at the head of the Union. He fills for the people the most important office in the district. He is the great man of the place. It must be so in other districts. The funds are con-tributed by the landowners, but they are distributed by public officers. Thus the Poor-law, which disposes of the landowners' property, also deprives them of the pleasure and the burden of distributing it themselves. A public officer is made, in fact, to administer their estates, and he stands between them and their compulsory bounties, securing the respect and confidence which they might and ought to have. The more the subject is examined, the more, I have no doubt,

SEARCHING FOR POTATOES IN A STUBBLE FIELD.

The evictions were numerous before the potato rot. It was not that great calamity, therefore, that superinduced them, or was the chief cause of the present desolation. The potato harvest and harvests of every kind have been lost many times before 1846, without reducing the people to their present misery. But that calamity threw the people at the mercy of the Government, and the Go-vernment used its power directly and indirectly, in accordance with the theory, to clear the land. Out-door relief was established in that season of distress, and relief altogether was coupled with the resignation of the land. The poor were required to give up their heritage, small though it were, for less than a mess of pottage. A law was passed, the 11 and 12 Vic. c. 47, entitled, "An Act for the Protection and Relief of the Destitute Poor Evicted from their Dwellings," which provided a means of evicting them, subjecting the landlords to the neces-sity of giving notice to Poor-law guardians, and to the share of a common burden. Under such stimuli and such auspices, the clearing process has gone on in an accelerated ratio, and Ireland is now dotted with ruined villages, and filled with a starving population, besieging the doors of crowded workhouses, and creeping into the halls and chambers of the deserted mansions of the nobility and gentry. A gentleman's mansion turned into a poor-house, is a fit emblem of the decay that a mistaken policy has brought on all classes. The system in-tended to relieve the poor, by making the landlords responsible for their welfare, has at once made it the interest, and therefore the duty, of the landlords to get rid of them. Extirpation is accordingly going forward at a rapid rate; and the evidence of that is now placed before the eyes and the understanding of the readers of the ILLUSTRATED LONDON NEWS.

I will give you, by-and-bye, some notices of driving for rent, of landowners impoverished by rates, and of bankrupt unions; but at present I must draw at-tention to some of the other Sketches I send. The Scalp of Brian Connor (here represented) has been already described; it is another illustration of the worse than pig-sty habitations of those who did live in the now roofless cottages. An-other Sketch follows (of Miss Kennedy), which shows that, amidst this world of wretchedness, all is not misery and guilt. Indeed, it is a part of our nature that the sufferings of some should be the occasion for the exercise of virtue in others. Miss Kennedy (about seven years old) is the daughter of Captain Kennedy, the Poor-law Inspector of the Kilrush Union. She is represented as engaged in her daily occupation of distributing clothing to the wretched children brought around her by their more wretched parents. In the front of the group I noticed one woman crouching like a monkey, and drawing around her the only rag she had left to conceal her nudity. A big tear was rolling down her cheek, with gratitude for the gifts the innocent child was distributing. The effect was heightened

SCALP OF BRIAN CONNOR, NEAR KILRUSH UNION-HOUSE.

This is the full page from the Illustrated London News which contained the drawing of the village of Moveen. The page also includes "Searching for potatoes in a stubble field", and "Scalp (small shelter in a ditch) of Brian Connor, near Kilrush Union house".
Image courtesy of the National Library of Ireland.

VILLAGE OF MOVEEN.

greatness—which are not to be found in a Poor-law and farms of a particular size—impressed law-makers and the landlords of Ireland with a strong desire to enlarge and consolidate farms, and clear them of the squatters and sub-tenants, who had formerly been permitted, if not encouraged. With a Poor-law, that desire could be safely acted on, and so it supplies a temptation and the means to carry eviction extensively into effect.

by the chilliness and dreariness of a November evening, and by the wet and mire in which the naked feet of the crowd were immersed. On Captain Kennedy being appointed to the Union, his daughter was much affected by the misery of the poor children she saw; and so completely did it occupy her thoughts, that, with the consent of her parents, she gave up her time and her own little means to relieve them. She gave away her own clothes—she was allowed to bestow part of her mother's—and she then purchased coarse materials, and made up clothing for children of her own age; she was encouraged by her father and some philanthropic strangers, from whom she received sums of money, and whose example will no doubt be followed by those who possess property in the neighbourhood; and she devoted herself with all the energy and perseverance of a mature and staid matron to the holy office she has undertaken. The Sketch will, I hope, immortalize the beneficent child, who is filling the place of a saint, and performing the duties of a patriot.

On all sides I hear praises of the amiable child and her excellent father, and this is not without a moral for the landlords. The public officers who are appointed to administer and control the relief of the poor, have it in their power to do much for the people. Mere kindness of manner, though they render no substantial assistance, endears them to the suffering crowd. Captain Kennedy is at once kind, charitable, and judicious. He is at the head of the Union. He fills for the people the most important office in the district. He is the great man of the place. It must be so in other districts. The funds are contributed by the landowners, but they are distributed by public officers. Thus the Poor-law, which disposes of the landowners' property, also deprives them of the pleasure and the burden of distributing it themselves. A public officer is made, in fact, to administer their estates, and he stands between them and their compulsory bounties, securing the respect and confidence which they might and ought to have. The more the subject is examined, the more, I have no doubt,

This drawing is of Moveen, a village near Kilrush in Co. Clare.

The people have been evicted and the roofs have been taken off the houses so that the people cannot return.

Image courtesy of the National Library of Ireland.

29

Repeal of the Corn Laws

There was no shortage of food in Ireland in 1845. Peel exaggerated the effects of the potato blight. He used this as a reason to repeal the Corn Laws and to allow cheap corn to be imported into the U.K. When the Corn Laws were repealed in June 1846, hundreds of thousands of Irish labourers were put out of work. This, together with the extra taxes imposed by the Poor Laws, was what caused the Irish people to starve in 1847.

Wheat and oats had been protected by high tariffs since the end of the war with Napoleon. A law was passed then that foreign corn could not be imported into the United Kingdom unless the price of home grown corn exceeded £80 a quarter. This Corn Laws Act was first introduced in June 1815. (The word corn included all grains, such as wheat, oats and barley.) This gave protection to the farmers in England and Ireland. The propaganda at the time blamed Napoleon for the need to impose the Corn Laws. Napoleon had made an attempt to blockade England so that no food could get through from Europe. The House of Commons decided that this should never happen again, and that the U.K. would be self-sufficient in food. They then put a tariff on foreign corn, to protect the farmer, so that he would be encouraged to grow corn for the home market.

This excuse was actually a spin on the real reason for the tax on foreign grain. Napoleon had been defeated at the battle of Waterloo, on 18 June 1815, by the Duke of Wellington and Prince Blucher of Prussia. The war with Napoleon had cost £20,000,000. The reason why the tariff was introduced after the battle of Waterloo was to pay for the expenses of that war. It was the landowners who would have to pay these extra taxes. In order to sweeten this extra tax, the Parliament passed the Corn Laws to give some assurance to the landowners that they would be protected in selling their corn on the home market, and they would make a profit.

Ireland had no quarrel with Napoleon. Unfortunately since 1801, Ireland no longer had any choice in the decisions about foreign policy. In 1800 the Irish parliament had voted itself out of existence, and agreed to join with the United Kingdom, in the Act of Union. Much bribery and corruption was involved, and many of those who voted for the Union were given titles and important jobs. Irish farmers and farm labourers benefitted from the Corn Laws, because Ireland was an agricultural country, more so than England. As long as the price of corn remained high, the Irish farm labourers would have employment.

However, in England there was opposition to the tax on corn. The factory owners said that if there were no tariffs on foreign corn, the workers would have cheaper bread, and they could then pay their factory workers less. They could sell their articles more cheaply. Of course there was also pressure from Canada and America to export their grain to England without having to pay high duty on it.

Some factory owners set up an Anti Corn Law League in England in 1839. They held rallies and collected signatures to put pressure on the government to remove the duty on foreign grain. The debate was seen as one of the rights of the factory worker in opposition to the privilege of the landed aristocracy. What was lost in the debate was that ordinary farm labourers would be put out of work if foreign corn was imported.

In 1843, the Economist magazine was founded in Edinburgh, as a magazine set up to publish propaganda for the repeal of the Corn Laws and for "Free Trade". The first editor of the Economist was James Wilson. He was backed in his enterprise by Lord Radnor, a liberal politician and member of the House of Lords, who paid for the first years' publication. The Anti Corn Law League, led by James Cobden, agreed to take 20,000 copies in the first year. The magazine then flourished. A spokesman for the Economist said recently on TV:-"We were for free trade since 1843 and it has always been a success." But there is no such thing as "Free Trade". It is a slogan which appears to suggest that goods will be cheaper, and that everyone will benefit. In reality it is the merchant class which reaps the benefit. The worker who has nothing but his labour is very often the loser. This is what happened in Ireland in June 1846, when the Corn Laws were repealed. This is what created the conditions in Ireland for a famine. The masses, who were already suffering under the imposition of a Poor Rate, were suddenly faced with unemployment and starvation. This was expressed clearly in the House of Commons in by Sir A Brooke, the M.P. for Fermanagh, in a debate on 6 March 1846:-

> The exports of Ireland to England, during the last year, in wheat, in barley, oatmeal, flour, and other articles of trade, amounted to nearly 5,000,000l. of money. He would ask, would it be to the advantage of this country that that vast sum should be transferred to America or to other countries? Would it be to the advantage of Ireland to have an amount of 5,000,000l. sent to foreign countries?[26]

But Peel was determined. He was ready to push through the Repeal of the Corn Laws, no matter what the consequences.

Karl Marx was a keen observer of the social and economic situation in Ireland. In 1867 he gave a lecture to the Communist Educational Association of German Workers in London, "On the Irish Question"[27]. He pointed to a number of causes for the Irish famine. He said the chief cause was the Repeal of the Corn Laws.

Peel used the excuse of the Potato blight to justify the Repeal of the Corn Laws

When Peel announced his decision to repeal the Corn Laws, he used the excuse of the potato blight in Ireland as a reason to do so. He said that there would be a famine in Ireland in 1846. For this reason it was necessary to remove the tariff from imported wheat. This excuse was disputed by a number of influential people. The Duke of Wellington was one of those. He said that he did not believe there was a famine in Ireland. There was no deficiency of food there. There was some potato blight, but arrangements could be made to meet the emergency.[28]

Lord Ashburton (Alexander Baring, of Baring's Bank), also expressed doubts about the existence of a famine in Ireland in 1846. He referred to the "supposed starving population". He said

> the best way of making provision for the wants of the people of Ireland would be, instead of opening the ports, to close them, in order to keep within the island the provisions which were already there, and assign them to the use of the supposed starving population".[29]

---

[26] House of Commons Debate, *Commercial Policy-Customs-Corn Laws.* 06 March 1846.

[27] Marx, Karl and Frederick Engels, R. Dixon (ed.), *Ireland and the Irish Question.* 1971 Moscow.

[28] House of Lords Debate, *Ministerial Explanation.* 26 January 1846.

[29] House of Lords Debate, *Corn Importation Bill-Adjourned Debate (Third Night).* 28 May 1846.

Yet Peel protested that the reason that he had to take the duty off imported corn was because the Irish were about to have a famine. He sent two experts over to Ireland, in October 1845, to report to him on the state of the potato harvest. These were Dr. Playfair and John Lindley. They reported that they travelled to Kildare and Wicklow, that is, they travelled to an area twenty miles around Dublin, and they said that the potato blight would get worse. In other words it was not yet worse. Their report referred to "The Prospect of approaching Scarcity." This was published in November 1845, well before unusual famine conditions prevailed in Ireland.

The M.P. for King's Lynn, Lord George Bentinck, ridiculed the report of Playfair and Lindley. He said that they picked the potatoes before they were ripe, and then they put them into a kiln to dry them. Then they buried them in a pit. They declared that the potatoes would be rotten in a few months. Of course potatoes would rot under those conditions.

Lord Bentinck also accused Sir Robert Peel of using the "pretended famine" as an excuse to repeal the Corn Laws.

> We are told by her Majesty's Ministers that there are four million of the Irish people on the brink of famine…If they honestly believe that there will be four million people requiring support for three months, they must know that it will require a million quarters of grain to feed them. They believe no such thing.[30]

Bentinck pointed out that Peel had sent for 100,000 quarters of maize to the United States. This amount would feed only 400,000 people. He doubted that Peel's Government thought that there was a need to feed millions of people in the summer of 1846. Bentinck said that Peel had betrayed the trust put in him when he promised the electorate in 1841 not to repeal the Corn Laws. Now, Peel was using the excuse of a famine in Ireland to change his mind, when the granaries in England and Ireland were full with wheat

> Good heavens, Sir! what a description of a country of famine! so completely choked that granary room is not to be found!! The quantity of grain in bond here consists of about 65,000 qrs. of wheat, 17,000 qrs. of barley, and 4,000 qrs. of oats, besides which we have about 40,000 to 45,000 qrs. of home wheat, chiefly very fine old English. And pray listen again, to this, Sir:— In fact, in place of the general outcry of 'famine,' we are literally labouring under repletion. Literally they say, Sir, labouring under repletion. To the quantity of wheat under bond, about 20,000 qrs., still on the passage, will soon be added, besides, a considerable quantity of barley and other grain.

Lord Bentinck also said that many influential people, including the Lord Lieutenant of Ireland, Lord Bessborough, reported that there was no widespread disease of the potato crop, and that Peel had suppressed these reports

> Well, then, I desire to know why Lord Bessborough's report to the Irish Government is suppressed? Is it because Lord Bessborough told both sides of the story, and that his report would not assist the present policy of Her Majesty's Ministers? I can also appeal to my noble Friend the Member for and Lieutenant of the county of Down; my noble Friend made his

---

[30] House of Commons Debate, *Customs and Corn Importation Report*. 26 March 1846.

report to the Irish Government. Why have we not had laid before us the report of my noble Friend the Lieutenant of the great county of Down? Then, again, there is my hon. and gallant Friend the Member for the county of Antrim, who was canvassing the county of Antrim throughout the month of December, and, feeling a deep interest in the prospects of the Irish people, lost no opportunity of making every possible inquiry as to the true state of the potato crop; and my hon. and gallant Friend has assured me that the invariable answer he received was—

"We have here and there a bad one, but we have no fault to find with the potato crop".

It is still a hotly debated question, even today, as to why Peel changed his mind about the repeal of the Corn Laws. He was accused of treachery and deceit, and his cabinet split over it. The repercussions were felt for many years afterwards, and it caused the dissolution of his party.

I would suggest that one reason he changed his mind was that there had been an attempt on his life in 1843. The attempt occurred in January 1843. The assassin, apparently acting alone, fired at point blank range into the back of the private secretary of Sir Robert Peel. The secretary, Edward Drummond, died a few days later in hospital. It was assumed that the assassin thought that he had followed Peel and had killed the wrong man. The assassin was immediately arrested. There were unusual circumstances in the manner in which this man MacNaughtan was treated. When he was arrested he had a bank receipt for £750 on him. His father claimed the money, and used it to pay for the legal team to defend his son. The son was convicted, but here another unusual event occurred. He was not condemned to death, as would have been expected. His was the first case ever of an assassin being judged guilty but insane, and sentenced to life imprisonment. There was speculation at the time that MacNaughtan was financed to assassinate Peel.

There are enough unexplained circumstances arising from this attempted assassination to suggest that Peel may have been frightened into agreeing to change his mind on the repeal of the Corn Laws.

At any rate, this is what he did.

It would seem that Peel did make some efforts to find out how the Repeal of the Corn Laws would affect the Irish. In November 1843 he set up a Commission to enquire into the "Occupation of Land" in Ireland. This was the Devon Commission. The report gave information on more questions than the occupation of land. It also gave an overview of the employment of the Irish population. It was clear that the majority of the Irish were dependent on employment in agriculture for a living. It would have been a reasonable assumption that if these agricultural workers were put out of work, there would be starvation in the land. The Devon Commission reported in February 1845. Peel had sufficient information available to him from the Devon report to know what would be the consequences to Ireland of the Repeal of the Corn Laws.

Another project which Peel set up before he introduced the Repeal of the Corn Laws was a Famine Relief Committee for Ireland. This Famine Relief Committee met in November 1845. It had on its board Sir Richard Routh, from the Commissariat of the Army, Colonel Harry Jones of the Board of Works in Ireland, Edward Twisleton, a new Poor Law Commissioner for Ireland, and Captain John Pitt Kennedy, who had been secretary to the Devon Commission.

In addition Peel appointed a commission to report on "Scarcity in Ireland". He even imported a small amount of Indian meal secretly. He also established a scheme to improve harbours in Ireland.

He then seized on the excuse of the potato blight and sent over Dr.Playfair and Mr.Lindley to report on whether the potato blight might cause a famine. The potato blight was first reported in Ireland in August 1845, so that it was not yet a great problem. On the other hand, the importation of foreign corn at a much reduced price would certainly present a problem for the Irish people.

When Peel set up the Commission of Inquiry into the potato blight, in September 1845, there was already research going on in Ireland to identify the cause of the blight. David Moore, the curator of the Royal Dublin Society's Botanic Gardens in Glasnevin in Dublin, was the first person to observe the blight on potatoes in Ireland, on 20 August 1845. He knew that it had already reached England, and he was on the alert to find when it would first appear in Ireland. In October of 1845, Moore gave a report to the Royal Dublin Society in which he suggested that the blight was caused by a fungus. He was in correspondence with an eminent English botanist, the Reverend Myles Berkeley, of Northamptonshire. Berkeley was in contact with French botanists, and was already watching for when the blight would reach England.

By July of 1846, David Moore had done significant research on the blight. He was convinced that the potato blight was caused by a parasitic fungus and he made recommendations to the Royal Dublin Society about steps which could be taken to save some of the potato crop. John Lindley disagreed with the findings of Moore and Berkeley. Lindley wrote in the "Gardeners Chronicle" that he disagreed with Berkeley and that the potato blight was caused by atmospheric conditions.

The research of David Moore has been referred to in a study by Dr. Earnest Charles Nelson, who wrote that Moore, like Berkeley, was hampered because he was opposed by a large number of people in influential positions.[31] Perhaps Moore and Berkeley fell foul of a greater political project, the Repeal of the Corn laws. Lindley had already received assistance from Sir Robert Peel in 1840, to save the Botanic Gardens in Kew. These had fallen into disrepair, and were only saved with the help of Sir Robert Peel. One good turn may have deserved another.

Peel was set on a course of repealing the Corn Laws. He knew it would cause devastation in Ireland. It would suit him to have a report from John Lindley to say that the potato blight would get worse. It was stated that John Lindley's report influenced the repeal of the 1815 Corn Laws, which had forbidden the import of cheap wheat from America. There may well have been a reason that the research in the Dublin Botanic Gardens was ignored.[32]

Peel set up some schemes to provide for the welfare of the Irish labourer who would be out of work when the Corn Laws would be repealed. Then he diverted attention away from the Corn Laws, and blamed the potato.

---

[31] E Charles Nelson, *Phytophthora infestans, or The Cause of the Calamity: potato blight in Ireland, 1845-1847, and the role of the Botanic Gardens Glasnevin.* Dublin 1995.

[32] Stearn, William T. The life, times and achievements of John Lindley., in Stearn (1998), The article states "In 1845, Lindley was part of a scientific commission set up by the Government to investigate potato blight and the Irish famine. The cause of the fungal disease was not known at the time and the weather was thought to be to blame. Although the commission was powerless to solve the problem, their report brought about the repeal of the 1815 Corn Laws which had forbidden the import of cheap wheat from America."

"I'M AFRAID YOU'RE NOT STRONG ENOUGH FOR THE PLACE, JOHN."

Queen Victoria hears from Lord John Russell that he cannot form a Government, in December 1845.
Russell was very small, and the drawing illustrates this.
Punch Cartoon 1845. Image courtesy of the National Library of Ireland.

"NEVER MIND LOSING THE FIRST HEAT: GO IN AND WIN.'

Robert Peel tells Lord Russell to go in to Parliament and Repeal the Corn Laws.
Punch cartoon 1846. Image courtesy of the National Library of Ireland.

Peel and Russell manipulated the Irish M.P.s into voting for the Repeal of the Corn Laws.

It was important for Sir Robert Peel to get the support of Irish M.P.s to repeal the Corn Law. The Bill had been brought before Parliament several times in the previous five years by the opposition, and had never secured a majority. There were resignations from Peel's cabinet in October 1845 when he announced his decision to repeal the Corn Laws. Peel would be in a stronger position to get the Repeal Bill passed if he were sure of the votes of Irish members of Parliament.

I suggest that Peel and Russell concocted a plan to persuade the Irish M.P.s to vote for the Bill. Their plan involved threatening the Irish with a Coercion Act. It then involved proposing a bargain with the Irish, that the Coercion Act would be withdrawn, if they voted for the repeal of the Corn Laws. My suggestion comes from a speech in the House of Commons made by Lord George Bentinck in a debate on the Coercion Bill for Ireland

> Sir, my right hon. Friend, in bringing this measure under the notice of this House, maintained a doctrine which I think much more likely to be written in letters of blood, for he bound up the question of the Corn Laws with the present one. He said, that unless (*if*) he could have prevailed on his Colleagues to accede to his free-trade measure as regards corn, he would not have introduced this bill"[33]

Bentinck said that Peel had made a bargain with the group who were opposed to the Coercion Act for Ireland, that if they agreed to the passing of the Repeal of the Corn Laws, then the Coercion Act would be defeated

> I should like to know, therefore, what this agrarian outrage has to do with the potato famine—and where is the justification for a Minister coming down to this House and declaring that unless we pass a free-trade measure we are not to obey Her Majesty's commands, by passing a measure for the protection of life in Ireland.

Peel played bad cop and introduced a Coercion act for Ireland. Russell played good cop and told the Irish that he would oppose it with all the power at his command. He gave a speech in Parliament in which he said he thought they were bound to consider also whether there were not measures that might be introduced that would lessen the causes of these crimes

> that he had himself read a newspaper account the other day, in which it was stated, that a whole village, containing 270 persons, had been razed to the ground, and the entire of that large number of individuals sent adrift on the high road, to sleep under the hedges, without even being permitted the privilege of boiling their potatoes, or obtaining shelter among the walls of the houses from which they had been dispossessed. When they took into consideration these crimes, he thought they should at the same time ask themselves whether the law of landlord and tenant in Ireland should not be improved and thus that these unconstitutional Bills,—for unconstitutional and harsh they were,—might hereafter be dispensed with.[34]

---

[33] *House of Commons Debate, Protection of Life (Ireland) Bill. 30 March 1846.*

[34] House of Commons Debate, *Protection of Life (Ireland) Bill. 06 April 1846.*

Oh perfidious Albion. As soon as Russell came into power, he withdrew the small amount of help for the starving people of Ireland which Peel had put in place. He introduced his own Coercion Bill in December 1847.

Lord Bentinck accused Peel of repealing the Corn Laws to make a small number of people rich. He said

> the practical result of the measure of the Government clearly would be to make a present to some two hundred, three hundred, or it might be four hundred individuals of upwards of half a million sterling.[35]

Lord George Bentinck also made a strong case for the Irish agricultural labourer. He said that the Repeal of the Corn Laws would put Irish agricultural labourers out of work, and would be a disaster for Ireland.

Lord Bentinck was supported by William Smith O'Brien in this debate. However, Peel resorted to aggressive tactics against William Smith O'Brien in the months leading up to the vote on the Corn Laws. He had Smith O Brien arrested by the Sergeant at Arms in the House of Commons, on 30 April 1846, and held in the House of Commons gaol for 23 days. The imprisonment was referred to in Parliamentary terms as being held "in durance vile". The reason Peel gave for this was that Smith O Brien was in contempt of Parliament because he had not attended a committee on railways, to which he had been assigned. O'Brien said that he wished to give all his attention to Irish affairs, and did not see why he should be part of a committee on railways for the U.K.[36]

Smith O Brien was released on 22 May 1846. This was because Daniel O Connell protested in Parliament that the Committee on Railways had not been properly convened, and therefore the arrest of O'Brien was null and void.(21 May 1846) His release came after the Bill for the Repeal of the Corn Laws had been passed in the House of Commons. The arrest of Smith O'Brien at this time removed an eloquent voice for Ireland in the debate.

A few days after the Repeal of the Corn Laws was passed in the House of Commons, and before it was passed by the House of Lords, the Coercion Bill for Ireland was brought again to the House of Commons. Lord Bentinck spoke against it. He said

> Is there any man in this House, is there any man in the country, who is fool enough to believe that Her Majesty's Government are in earnest with their Life and Property Protection Bill?

In this speech Lord Bentinck accused Sir Robert Peel of duplicity. He also accused Peel of hounding his uncle, the Prime Minister George Canning to death. He said

> we hear from the right hon. Baronet himself—that it would have been base and dishonest in him, and inconsistent with his duty to his Sovereign, if he had concealed his opinions after he had changed them; but I have lived long enough, I am sorry to say, to remember, and to remember with sorrow—with deep and heartfelt sorrow—the time when the right hon. Baronet chased and hunted an illustrious relative of mine to death; and when he stated that

---

[35] House of Commons Debate, *Foreign Grain in bond.* 11 February 1846.

[36] House of Commons Debate, *Mr. W. Smith O'Brien serving on Committees.* 30 April 1846.

he could not support his Ministry…[37]

Bentinck's case was that in 1828 Peel refused to support Prime Minister Canning in a Bill to give Catholic Emancipation to the Irish, and that he caused a major division in the government, which led to the sickness and death of Canning. Canning was in office only for 119 days as Prime Minister. He died suddenly on 8 August 1828. He was 57 years of age. There were various explanations given for his death. One explanation was that he had caught a chill at the funeral of Frederick, Duke of York in January 1828, and that he had never really recovered.

Peel took the accusation seriously. On 19 June 1846 he took time in the House of Commons to answer the accusations of Lord Bentinck. The item is called "Sir Robert Peel's explanation" in the House of Commons debates.[38] Peel said that he had been denounced as a garbler, and mutilator and suppressor of the truth. It was not true that he had been in favour of Catholic emancipation in 1825, and had then changed his mind. He denied the accusations of Lord Bentinck. It was clear that Peel was angry at the accusations of Lord Bentinck.

On 15 May 1846, 42 Irish members voted with Lord Russell in favour of the Bill for the Repeal of the Corn Laws. The vote was 327 Ayes, and 229 Noes. The vote was carried by a majority of 98. The Bill was then sent to the House of Lords for their approval.

On 25 June 1846, the House of Lords approved of the Repeal of the Corn Laws, and the Bill was passed. On that same night, Lord Russell and his followers voted against the Coercion Act for Ireland. The vote was 219 Ayes, and 292 Noes. The vote was lost by a majority of 73. The Coercion Act was lost, and the government of Sir Robert Peel fell. There was no election. The Queen sent for Lord Russell and asked him to form a government, which he did.

The effect of this Act on Ireland was that the Irish farmers could no longer sell their grain at a profit. They lost their trade in corn. There was a sudden drop in the amount exported from Ireland after 26 June 1846. Two million quarters of corn which were held in bonded warehouses in England were suddenly released on the English market. There was a huge jump in supplies in July 1846, from 79,546 total imports of grain in June to 2,287,285 in July. The amount of corn exported from Ireland to Britain dropped by a half.[39]

A new state of economic affairs now existed in Ireland. As Lord Bentinck had stated, and Peel would have known, hundreds of thousands of Irish small farmers lost their livelihoods.

No wonder Daniel O Connell was disillusioned. Too late he realised how badly he had been treated by Lord Russell. In 1847 he travelled to Rome to make an appeal to the Pope. He has been seen as an old man on a lonely mission of despair. It is more likely that he was aware of the political manoeuverings of Lord Russell and that he went to persuade the Pope not to accept English interference in the affairs of Ireland. It was tragic that he died in Genoa, before he reached Rome. He died on 15 May 1847 at the age of 71.

There is a sad postscript also to the career of Lord Bentinck. He died in mysterious circumstances two years after the Repeal of the Corn Laws. On 21 September 1848, Lord Bentinck set

---

[37] House of Commons Debate, *Protection of Life (Ireland) Bill.* 08 June 1846.

[38] House of Commons Debate, *Sir R. Peel's explanation.* 19 June 1846.

[39] Parliamentary Papers, Returns relating to the import and export of wheat 19 Jan. 1847. (Mr. Parker)

out for a walk from his family home of Welbeck Abbey in Nottingham to visit Charles Pierrepont, Earl Manvers, six miles away, at Thoresby Hall. When he didn't arrive his servant went out to find him. He was lying face down in the ground, dead. He was 46 years of age. There was no satisfactory cause given for his death. It is somewhat suspicious that it was known where he was going, and that it was known that he was alone, at the time of his death. There were many rumours around the circumstances of his death. Some said that he died from an attack of apoplexy. There was speculation that it was suicide. There were some who said that it was murder, and that a notorious poisoner called William Palmer was responsible. It would be hard to prove that Sir Robert Peel was remotely responsible, but that strange justification of his behaviour in the House of Commons showed that there were considerable tensions between Sir Robert Peel and Lord Bentinck.

ANOTHER VERSION OF JOHNNY GILPIN.

AWAY went BENTINCK, neck or nought,
'Gainst every timid Whig;
They little dreamt when he set out,
He would run such a rig.

Some Irish Members cheer'd him on,
Protectionists and all
Cried out, "Go at it, GEORGE; well done!"
As loud as they could bawl.

Away went BENTINCK, who but he
Could run such pace around?
He carries weight, he rides a race
For sixteen million pound.

Lord George Bentinck pleaded with Russell to invest in railways in Ireland instead of wasting the money on Relief Works. The figure 0f £16,000,000 in the background is the amount which Lord Russell said was the cost which the loss of the potato crop caused to Ireland. He exaggerated the figures. Bentinck bred racehorses so "the stable mind" is written on the engine. Punch cartoon 1847.

Image courtesy of the National Library of Ireland.

41

JUSTICE TO IRELAND.

"She gave them some Broth without any Bread,
Then whipp'd them all Round, and sent them to Bed."

Peel threatened the Irish with a Coercion Act if they did not vote for the Repeal of the Corn Laws in 1846.
Punch cartoon 1846.
Image courtesy of the National Library of Ireland.

THE BAD BOY WHO DIDN'T CARE.

Mr. Speaker.—"THERE, MASTER O'BRIEN, GO INTO THE CELLAR, AND DON'T COME OUT TILL YOU KNOW HOW TO BEHAVE YOURSELF."

William Smith O'Brien was held in the House of Commons prison for 23 days during the time that the Corn Law Repeal Bill was passed. Punch Cartoon 1846.

Image courtesy of the National Library of Ireland.

Famine Relief Schemes

The beginning of the horror, Black 47.

As soon as Lord John Russell became Prime Minister, in July 1846, things got dramatically worse for the Irish. He closed down all the Relief Schemes, which had been started by Sir Robert Peel. He gave notice that with effect from 15 August 1846, all works on these schemes would cease. He closed down all the committees which distributed relief throughout Ireland. He accused them of giving relief to their friends and supporters. Then, on 30 August 1846, he introduced the most disastrous relief scheme that was ever devised by the ingenuity of man. He spent more than £4,848,235 sterling in employing men, women, and children, on breaking stones and making roads to nowhere. This scheme was introduced in a Bill which became known as the "Labour Rate Act". It was passed on 30 August 1846. It was called the Labour Rate Advances Act, 9 & 10 Vict., c. 107.

The man who administered the Labour Rate Act for Ireland was Henri Labouchere. Henri Labouchere, Baron Taunton (1798-1869) was appointed Chief Secretary for Ireland by Lord John Russell. He held the position from July 1846 to July 1847.

Labouchere was from the banking family of Sir Francis Baring. His mother was the daughter of Sir Francis Baring. His wife was the grand daughter of Sir Francis Baring. Henri Labouchere's father was Pierre Cesar Labouchere, from the banking firm of Hope and Co. of Rotterdam. His father was a partner of the Baring family in their banking operations in America. Henri Labouchere was a banker through and through.

When he became Chief Secretary for Ireland, he changed the system by which the government gave aid to Ireland. All the money which he arranged to give to Ireland was by way of a loan and not a grant. It would all have to be repaid. It was advanced from the Consolidated Funds, that is, from the National debt. It was long term money for capital projects. In the language of government administrators, it came from a "different envelope" to that of giving grants for emergency aid. This money did not count as an annual expense, it was treated as a capital expense for budget purposes. This would make it more appealing for a banker such as Henri Labouchere to advance money as a loan, not a grant, to the Irish.

The aid which Russell and Labouchere proposed in the "Labour Rate Act" was aid for the poor who would give their labour in return for food and wages. No food was to be given for free. The Act set out that a rate would be imposed on the Irish people to pay for this "labour". This would be a "Labour" rate. That is, this would be an extra rate which would be added to the Poor rate. It was an extra rate which the Guardians of the workhouses then had to collect and deliver to the Government. The amount of the Poor Rates rose dramatically as a result.

The speeches of Lord Russell in the House of Parliament in January 1847 would suggest that the Irish poor were being relieved with great generosity, but this was not the truth. The truth was that the government at this period from August 1846 until January 1847 did very little. This is the cause of the "Great Calamity", which has been fudged over and ignored for decades. The truth is that this was a time when outdoor relief could have saved the people from starving, but this was not given.

There was an additional proviso which made the "Labour Rate" Act even more useless. It was that the work done must not benefit any one landlord rather than another. Whatever chance there might have been that the "Labour Rate" might have provided some useful return was doomed by this condition. The work which was considered suitable consisted in the main of building roads or draining land. Often land was drained, but the adjoining land was not, so that the drainage was ineffective. The roads which were built, led into the middle of bogs, and then stopped. A vast amount of money was spent in administering the schemes, and paying overseers and engineers to make decisions on which works would be done.

It was also decided that the labourers on the works should be paid less than the customary wage, so that they would not leave their normal agricultural work to work on relief schemes. As a result, the average wage on the Relief schemes was 10 pennies a day. This was not enough to buy one meal for a family. The restrictions and regulations which went along with the scheme were sufficient to make sure that it would be useless as a means of providing food for the poor.

The Board of Works records of the Relief Schemes are in the National Archives of Ireland, in Dublin. A typical record of one of the schemes shows that the labourers needed wheelbarrows, pick axes for breaking stones, and donkeys to carry the loads. A page from a Board of Works ledger for 1847 showed that the amount spent on Relief Works from March 1 1847 to 12 June 1847 was £2,109,522. When this sum is compared with the cost of building 130 workhouses at that time, which was £1,200,000, it is clear that this was a very large sum to spend on casual labour for fifteen weeks.

Most of this work started in the winter of 1846-1847. A million Irish people were employed making roads or draining land in the depths of winter, in the freezing cold and driving rain. Many women and children joined the relief schemes to earn a few more pennies. A total of £4,848,000 million pounds was spent on these works. The schemes were so numerous, and the administration of the works was so difficult, that it defies belief that any sane administration would have thought of administering relief in this way.

The Irish Board of Works was given the job of supervising almost one million labourers on small public works throughout Ireland. The fact that the Board of Works had to oversee all of these people meant that they suddenly had to recruit a very large number of supervisors. These supervisors had to be trained. The Head of the Board of Works from 1845 to 1850 was Colonel Harry Jones of the Royal Engineers. His solution was to appoint officers of the English army to become inspectors on the Board of Works Schemes. They were all Army Captains or Majors, many of them from the Corps of Engineers.

There was a long delay before any of the relief schemes could be started. Grand Juries had to be set up in each Union to decide what work should be done. The Board of Works officials then judged if the schemes were suitable. When they were approved, the work could commence. This delay may have been intentional on the part of the government, as there was a financial crisis in the Bank of England during this time. There had also been delays in implementing previous relief schemes. There is a note in the National Archives marked confidential, which is from Dublin Castle, from the Office of the Lord Lieutenant, Lord Bessborough, which supports this view. The letter, dated 18 March 1846, said "I am directed by the Lord Lieutenant to inform you that in consequence of the representations of the Scarcity Commissioners of the insufficiency of the sum of public money placed at the disposal of the Board of Works... you are authorised to receive memorials for grants and to recommend the sanction of the Treasury without regard to the limited amount of the sums which Parliament has hitherto provided".[40]

While this was happening, people were dying. The number of people who were going to the workhouses doubled in the period from April 1846 to April 1847. A table from the Thirteenth report of the Poor Law Commissioners shows that the number in the workhouses in the week ending 4 April 1846 was 50,861. A year earlier it was 41,651. One year later, in the week ending 10 April 1847, it was 104,455. The table also gives the number who died in each week in the workhouses. In the week ending 4 April 1846, 159 died. In the week ending 10 April 1847, 2,613 died. The number who died outside the workhouses is not known, but it can be at least as many as those who died within the workhouses.[41]

The Relief works had taken place at a time when men could have been preparing the ground for planting crops, and this time had been spent on public works instead. The potato crop was not diseased in 1847, but very few potatoes were sown. This increased the hunger and misery of the people in 1847.

The operation of the Labour Rate Act caused the devastation and decimation of the population of Ireland in the winter of 1846-1847. It created the conditions for the disease and death of the year 1847, "Black 47". This was a direct result of the policies of Lord Russell and his chief secretary Henri Labouchere. Years later, the Irish M.P. George Henry Moore referred to this scheme as one totally unsuited to relieving famine, and a huge mistake. He referred to the fact that the Government in 1853 wished to recoup £2.231,000 (or half of the cost) of the Labour Rate Act. He said:-

> that the mode of relief under which the greater part of these charges has occurred, was, in itself, utterly unsuited to meet the exigency with which it had to cope: that it was adopted, and set on foot, after due and timely warning of its inadequacy and inevitable failure: That it was persevered in, long after it had been proved and admitted to be not only inadequate and unfit for the preservation of life, but destructive to property, and subversive of society itself: That when it was found impossible to expend these loans on works of public utility, it was stipulated, as the next best test of their fitness, that such works should be at least useless to those who were ultimately to pay for their execution: that not only were works so executed no test of destitution, and no fit mode of relieving famine, but that they enticed multitudes from their regular employment; and while they generated disease and death among the feeble and infirm, they deteriorated the value of property, and shortened the future means of human subsistence, by greatly diminishing the agricultural labours that would have otherwise contributed to the coming harvest.[42]

In 1853 the government agreed with the opinion of George Henry Moore. After an interval of six years, the judgement of the House of Commons was that this scheme had been a disaster.

In 1847, there was no one who could stop Lord Russell imposing his policies on the Irish people.

----

[40] National Archives of Ireland, *Relief Ctte distress (confidential)*. OP/1846/197.

[41] Parliamentary Papers, *Thirteenth Annual Report of the Commissioners for administering the laws for the relief of the Poor 1847.* (816) Vol. XXVII. Page 26. *This page is reproduced in the Appendices.*

[42] House of Commons Debate, *Consolidated Annuities (Ireland)*. 07 April 1853.

Further relief schemes 1847

There were two further relief schemes which were introduced by Labouchere during his time as Chief Secretary for Ireland. These were the scheme under the Labouchere letter, and the Temporary Relief Scheme of General Burgoyne.

The Labouchere Letter

A number of landowners appealed to Labouchere in September 1846 to change the provisions of the Labour Rate Act. They said that it would be better if they could employ labourers on their own estates, to improve their own farms. This would be a more effective use of the money to be spent on relief. Labouchere did not change the Labour Rate Act, but he did set up a loan scheme to assist these landowners. A total amount of £290,000 was advanced and repaid over ten years. It was not significant as a relief scheme. However, there are many famine relief walls around estates in Ireland which are a lasting tribute to the landlords who borrowed under this scheme. Perhaps they saved some people from starvation.

Temporary Relief Scheme (Burgoyne Scheme)

There were hundreds of thousands employed on the public works in 1847, and the cost was enormous. It could not continue. In January 1847 Lord Russell and Labouchere announced that the public works scheme would be scaled down. This took several months. In the meantime, they announced a new scheme. It was a Temporary Relief Scheme, known as the Burgoyne Scheme. It was named after Colonel John Fox Burgoyne, who administered it. Russell and Labouchere now proposed that the embargo on outdoor relief would be lifted for a temporary period, and that people would be given relief in food, without having to live in the workhouse. There were restrictions on this outdoor relief. It would only be given to a widow with two legitimate children, or old and infirm people. Able bodied men and women were still excluded from this scheme.

The "Famine Pot" became a feature of the Burgoyne Temporary Relief Scheme. Relief committees were given boilers and food to cook in them. The boilers were manufactured in the Royal Navy Arsenal at Woolwich. A minute from Charles Trevelyan to Commissary General Sir Richard Routh confirms this. The minute said:-

> I am disappointed at the Ordnance iron pots being too small, but I have taken immediate steps to supply the deficiency; have purchased eight or ten boilers holding from 60 to 100 gallons each, to be put on board the two vessels bound for Killybegs; have requested the Admiralty to have new boilers made as fast as possible at Woolwich, at the rate of 20 or 30 a week; and have set on foot active enquiries at the principal iron foundries, from the answers to which it appears that the Carron and other foundries are fully employed and could not undertake to make a delivery of new boilers in less than two months; but we are in hopes that we shall be more successful at the foundries...[43]

These "Famine Pots" are now treasured as relics of the famine, and people fondly believe that they were the means of feeding the starving Irish, and the instrument of benevolent charity. They

---

[43] Parliamentary Papers, *Correspondence from January to March 1847 relating to the measures adopted for the relief of distress in Ireland.* Commissariat series. Second part. Page image 41 of 246 (1847(796)).

were not. They were just as much a symbol of repression of the Irish by the Government administration as the image of the potato was. The boilers do not appear to have been widely used. The poor people were not in one place to receive hot food at the one time, as would be the men who were in the navy. The Distress Records show that people walked for miles and got dry food, such as a quarter stone of oatmeal, to bring home to their families, not hot soup.

There are many heart breaking stories, in every district, of starving people walking miles to relief distribution points to collect some food for their families. In Bawnboy in Co. Cavan, local people remember the grave of the widow woman from Glengevlin who walked to Bawnboy for food for herself and her children and who died on the way home on the side of a ditch. There are many similar stories throughout Ireland.

Lord Russell introduced this new "Temporary Relief Scheme" with much fanfare and publicity. In March 1847, a French chef called "Le Soyer" was brought over to Dublin and gave a demonstration of how a nutritious soup could be made from very few ingredients. Unfortunately the soup which was served to the starving poor did not have the same ingredients. There were complaints that it was bad for people's health. It was so liquid it caused diarrhea and doctors complained that it thereby weakened people.

The people today might as well have these famine pots and put them in places connected with the famine, as they own them, and their ancestors have paid for them. The money spent under the Burgoyne Relief scheme all had to be repaid by the Irish rate payer. A sum of £900,000 was added to the rate to be collected by the Guardians of the workhouses. The Government decided that all of the money for the Burgoyne Relief scheme must be paid within one year, that is, before the end of 1848.

By mid-August 1847 it was announced that the Burgoyne temporary relief scheme was finished. It had lasted four and a half months. From then on nothing more was done for the poor until November 1847 when the new Poor Law came into operation. All of these Relief Schemes increased the amount to be charged on the rates. The amount of rates which were imposed on the landowners in 1847 was almost seven times that which had been charged in 1843. A table from the Cavan newspaper, the Anglo Celt, of Friday 13 April 1849, shows that two rates were levied in 1847. One of about one shilling in the pound was levied in January 1847, and a second, of about 3 shillings in the pound, was levied in December, to pay for the Burgoyne scheme. [44]

Many tenants could not pay this, and their landlord became responsible for paying the rates for all his tenants who held land under £4 in value.

Labouchere's term of office as Chief Secretary was ruinous for Ireland. It precipitated the slow starvation of the Irish people, and left them weakened, so that when typhoid and cholera appeared, the population did not have the strength to resist it.

---

[44] Anglo Celt, Cavan, Friday 13 April 1849. *This table is reproduced in the Appendices.*

CONSOLATION FOR THE MILLION.—THE LOAF AND THE POTATO.

This cartoon from Punch, in 1847, points out that the potato crops were not affected by blight in 1847. The loaf of bread is saying to the potato : "Well ! old fellow I am delighted to see you looking so well- Why they said you had the Aphis Vastater."

and the potato replies : "All humbug sir never was better in my life, thank Heaven."

Many other sources throw doubt on the prevalence of potato blight in 1847. . Sir John Burgoyne mentioned this in a letter sent to the Irish newspapers on 6 Oct. 1847 "Although there has been no potato blight this year, there were too few potatoes sown."

Image courtesy of the National Library of Ireland.

This is a famine pot which is in Bawnboy Workhouse. The large iron pots were first brought to Ireland in 1847. They were made in the Navy Arsenal at Woolwich. Their purpose was to hold a large amount of soup to feed the starving Irish. They were not much used, as the population would have to walk miles each day to get the soup. Instead, the people walked once a week to places where the relieving officers gave out dry food, such as oatmeal. The cost of these pots was charged to the Irish, and added to the amount which was to be paid under the Poor Rates.

Photo, D. M. Headen

THE EFFECTS OF TIGHT LACING ON THE OLD
LADY OF THREADNEEDLE STREET.

This cartoon from Punch in 1847 shows Sir Robert Peel squeezing the corset of the Old Lady of Threadneedle Street (the Bank of England). In October 1847 the Bank suspended the gold standard to prevent the collapse of the Bank of England. (Bank Charter is written on a poster behind Peel). This pressure came at the height of the famine in Ireland. It made matters worse.

Image courtesy of the National Library of Ireland.

The Bank of England crisis in 1847

There was a slight excuse for the policies of Lord Russell and Labouchere in deciding that all relief should be in the form of loans, which must be repaid, rather than in giving grants. This slight excuse was that there was a financial crisis in England at the time and it looked as if the Bank of England would become insolvent. The reason for the crisis was the repeal of the Corn Laws. Many people borrowed money to import corn cheaply from America. They had been told often enough that the Irish people would have no potatoes, and that they would buy wheat. The speculators imagined that they would make a large profit. However, when the corn had to be paid for, in the spring of 1846, the money to pay for it had to be shipped to America in the form of gold bullion. The coffers of the bank of England began to empty at an alarming rate.

English banks were then on the gold standard. They could only issue notes to the value of £14,000,000 above the gold and silver bullion which they held in their vaults. It was Sir Robert Peel who introduced the law linking the currency to the gold standard, in 1844, in the Bank Charter Act 1844 (7 and 8 Vict. Cap 32).

As more and more gold flowed out of the country to America to pay for the imported corn, the Bank of England had to limit the amount of bank notes which it had in circulation. The consequence of this was that Lord Russell did not have as much money to distribute in aid as he might otherwise have had. In May 1846, the amount of gold bullion which was held in the Bank of England was £11,633,619. By 24 April 1847 this had become £7,120,006. The amount of currency in circulation in May 1846 was £27,520,215 and at the end of April 1847 it was £22,594,140. [45]

Lord Russell and the government tried to keep it secret, but by the autumn of 1847 it had reached a crisis point. Russell and his government suspended the gold standard, and started printing paper money. The Bank was saved, but only by the actions of the government in relaxing the laws to accommodate the banks. It was a strategy which has been used in recent times also.

There was a debate in the House of Commons in November 1847 on the "commercial distress". Thomas Baring, the M.P. for Cornwall and a member of the Baring Banking family, made a speech in which he accused Lord Russell of creating the conditions for merchants to speculate in importing corn. He said Russell exaggerated the lack of food in Ireland, and convinced merchants to speculate in corn because they thought they would make a vast profit. Baring said

> But he would ask who were the individuals who encouraged these exaggerated alarms? He could not say that the right hon. Gentleman or that the Government were free from blame, because he must say that the measures which were taken by the Government were sufficient to persuade the commercial men of the country that there were no available means by which they could bring a sufficient supply of food into the country. In 1847, the noble Lord said that the failure of the potato crop amounted to a loss of 16,000,000l. sterling. What were the measures taken to supply this deficiency? The navigation laws were suspended—their suspension was prolonged in June—and what individual, therefore, could imagine but that those who had access to the best sources of information were the parties who best knew what were the wants of the country, and therefore they risked their all, and bought what corn they

---

[45] Parliamentary Papers, Bank of England Bank notes. *A return of the notes, securities, bullion, &c. at the Bank of England, as published in the gazette.* 1847 (360).

could, even at the most enormous prices, that they might be able to meet the demand which, as they supposed, the Government had so wisely foreseen. [46]

Then Baring gave a summary of his opinion of the Banking act of 1844, which could have been a textbook explanation of John Maynard Keynes' policies during the New Deal. He said that the Government must have the opportunity to print more money when there is pressure on the economy. Baring also referred to the fact that there had been too much speculation in corn. There had also been over speculation in railways and this had stretched the credit of the banks. However, the money used for investing in railways did not leave the country, so it did not cause the crisis.

Earlier in the year, in April 1847, there had been a drop in the amount of gold bullion held in the Bank of England, and this almost caused a crisis in the capacity of the bank to issue paper money and to keep the system running. However, at the last minute, a sum of £400,000 came into the coffers of the bank in gold bullion. The Chancellor of the Exchequer Wood said in May 1847

> The last return shows a very much improved condition. Since last Saturday the Bank has received 400,000l. in gold and silver bullion, and the circulation of the country has been increased, nearly that amount of notes having been issued in exchange for gold and silver.[47]

By a coincidence, this is approximately the amount of money which was raised in the appeal for help for the Irish, which was put out by the British Relief Association in January 1847. In October the situation again became critical. Lord Russell announced that the Government would abandon the gold standard for a temporary period. This stopped the panic and the crisis eased.

There was a parliamentary inquiry into the financial crisis. It was held in secret. The report of the inquiry was published in 1848. It was called "A secret inquiry into the causes of the commercial distress in 1847." The committee of inquiry included Lord Russell, Lord Bentinck, Thomas Baring M.P., and Henri Labouchere. Amongst the people who were interviewed were the former director of the Bank of England, Mr. Herries, the banker, Samuel Loyd Jones, the banker, Thomson Hankey and the banker, Baron Lionel de Rothschild. One of the conclusions of the inquiry was that the banks had lent too much money to speculators to buy corn from America, and to invest in railway stocks.[48]

---

[46] House of Commons Debate, *Commercial Distress.* 30 November 1847.

[47] House of Commons Debate, *The Monetary Pressure.* 07 May 1847.

[48] Parliamentary Papers, *Supplemental appendix to reports from the Secret Committee on Commercial Distress.* 1847-48 (395).

MRS. THREADNEEDLE'S SOOTHING SYRUP.

54 This illustration from Punch shows a Banker offering £3,000,000 to Lord Russell to ease the banking crisis. "Did it have a nasty panic, Here then, Here then!!!" Sir Robert Peel is sitting on the knee of Lord Russell. Punch 1847.
Image courtesy of the National Library of Ireland.

The British Association

On 1 January 1847, a group of bankers met in the London home of Baron Lionel de Rothschild. They set up an Association to raise money for the starving Irish, and also for those in distress in the Highlands of Scotland. They sent out an appeal all over the world to ask for donations. The people who gave money would have been upset to know that the money they contributed was mainly given to the workhouses in Ireland. But first it was used to save the Bank of England.

John Mitchel accused the British Association of using the money they raised for Ireland for their own purposes. He was correct. The money went straight into English banks. It helped to bridge a liquidity crisis which occurred because people were speculating in buying corn. Mitchell said

> it was England that "sent round the hat over all the globe, asking a penny for the love of God to relieve the poor Irish," and constituting herself the agent of all that charity, took all the profit of it.[49]

Mitchel, (1815-1875), was a writer and political activist and a member of the Young Irelanders' movement.

By good fortune, the minute book of the dealings of the British Relief Association has been preserved in the National Library of Ireland. The secretary of the Association was Stephen Spring Rice, the son of Lord Monteagle of Brandon. It was he who kept the records of the Association. It gives a very interesting insight into their work.[50] The remarkable thing about the British Relief Association was the number of bankers who were on the committee. All the people who were called to the secret banking inquiry held in November 1847 were there. Thomson Hankey, the banker from Manchester was there, Raikes Currie of Curries Bank, and Abel Smith, of the Bank of Smith Paynes and Smiths were there. Thomas Baring, M.P. was there. These were all men who were very aware of the drain which had taken place on the currency, when gold bullion had been shipped to America.

It was decided at the first meeting of the British Association that an appeal would be made for funds to help the poor in Ireland and Scotland, and that Queen Victoria would be asked to join her name to the appeal. It was also arranged that she would give a donation of £2,000. The minutes of 4 January 1847 had a minute which said

> Read:- a Letter from the Right Honourable Lord John Russell M.P., announcing that her most gracious Majesty the Queen, had been pleased to order her name to be inserted as a donor of two thousand pounds towards the object of the fund.

The amount of money which was raised by the British Association has been given by Charles Trevelyan in his book "the Irish Crisis", as £434,784. The money which was given by so many donors was all lodged in the Bank of England. Every now and then, it is recorded in the minutes that some of this money would be transferred into the bank of one of the committee members. An example is the entry for Saturday, April 24, 1847, when £10,000 was transferred into the bank of Smith Payne and Smith

---

[49] John Mitchel, *The Last Conquest of Ireland (Perhaps)*. Lynch, Cole & Meehan New York 1873.

[50] Somebody called E.P. O'Connor bought this manuscript minute book for 10/6 shillings in 1945 and presented it to the National Library. My hat off to him.

> That a sum of ten thousand pounds be transferred from the account at the Bank of England to the drawing account of Messers. Smith, Payne and Smiths. Signed Lionel Rothschild.[51]

It was a resourceful plan to have money making its way back to the Bank of England instead of flowing out to America to pay for wheat. The money was all collected by the agents of the British government in foreign countries. In the British Dominions, it was the Governor Generals who collected the money, and sent it back to England. In Washington, it was the British Ambassador who collected the money. It is he who recorded that the Choctau Indians had given a sum of £179, which was lodged with him.

At an early stage, on 7 January 1847, it is recorded in the minute book that one of the Rothschild family, Sir Moses Montefiore, offered to go to Ireland to see for himself the problems which affected Ireland. His offer was accepted. Montefiore (1784-1885) was an interesting figure[52]. His father was a broker of gold bullion, in London. He was a brother in law of Nathan Mayer Rothschild (1777-1836). In 1825 Montefiore had become a director of the Provincial Bank of Ireland. It was a bank which was set up to do business with Catholic clients, in competition with the National Bank of Ireland, which was seen as a bank for Protestants. In 1860 he was a leading figure in the Zionist movement, and made an effort to buy Jerusalem from the Turks, who occupied it at the time.

It is also in this minute book that the Count Paul de Strzelecki is mentioned for the first time in connection with Ireland. It is recorded in the minutes of Wednesday, 28 January 1847, that Samuel Jones Loyd suggested that Strzelecki would be a suitable person to send to Ireland to supervise the distribution of aid there. The minute said "The chairman (Thomas Baring, M.P.) reported to the committee that he had an interview with Mr. S. Jones Loyd, a member of the committee, who had introduced to himself and Mr. Kingscote, the Count Strzlitzski, a Polish gentleman of extensive travel, who had offered at his own personal charges gratuitously to visit Ireland with a view to being useful to the Committee".

The minutes said "Consideration deferred". Later he was invited to meet the committee. The note in the minute book said

> It was Agreed that a letter be written to C. E. Trevelyan, Esq., requesting that the Count Strelitsky might be put officially in communication with Commissiary General Sir Randolph Routh. That the Count Strelitsky be requested to proceed immediately to Dublin, and after putting himself in communication with Commissary General Sir Randolph Routh and consulting with him to proceed to the counties of Donegal, Mayo and Sligo, reporting from time to time to the Committee as to the condition of their populations.

He was given instructions which were set out by Trevelyan, and told to report to him. The instructions had been given previously to another agent of the British Association, Captain Hanston.

---

[51] National Library of Ireland. *Minute Book of the British Association for the Relief of Distress in Ireland and Scotland.* M.S. 2022. Saturday April 24 1847.

[52] Montefiore was one of the people who was looking to relocate the Jewish people who were being persecuted in Eastern Europe and elsewhere. He eventually bought land in the Holy Land. Perhaps he had an idea of settling some Eastern European Jewish people in Ireland.

The instructions advised both men to keep Trevelyan informed of any information which might be of interest to him.

The appointment of Strzelecki was just one aspect of the work of the British Association. Its main object was to raise money throughout the world, and to distribute it in Ireland. For most of the time when this was being done, there was a financial crisis in England, and many banks failed.

In October 1847, just before the government of Lord Russell decided to suspend the backing of the currency by the gold standard, the British Association made one more appeal. Queen Victoria again sent out a letter asking for money for the starving Irish. This appeal was not so successful. A few weeks later, on 31 October 1847, Russell announced the emergency suspension of the gold standard. The announcement was enough to lift the sense of panic which had pervaded the stock markets. Within a few weeks the Bank of England was again restored to the gold standard, and commerce returned to normal. Many banks and businesses had become bankrupt during 1847, but the Bank of England was saved.

Much of the money collected by the British Association was eventually paid to Boards of Guardians of the workhouses which were most in distress. Some of it was spent on giving meals to school children. The main agent in Ireland for the British Association had become the Count Paul de Strzelecki. It was he who recorded the statistics of the number of children who were feed by the donations of the British Association. It is evident from the reports in other documents relating to Ireland that he greatly exaggerated the figures. He may have had another reason for being in Ireland. It is possible that he was acting as a secret agent for the government of Lord Russell.

Count Strzelecki the Spy?

I suggest that it is possible that Count Strzelecki was a spy for the Government of Lord Russell. Although he was acting as an agent for the British Association, this may have been a cover for his real work.

He was in Ireland from February 1847 to Sept 1848. While he was there he was in charge of a staff of 52 people, who acted as "assistant temporary inspectors" of Poor Law Unions. Thirty two of these were Army Captains or Majors or Officers of the Royal Navy. They all reported to Strzelecki. A list of their names is given in the First Report of the Poor Law Commissioners for Ireland. They included, in the Distressed Unions, Captain Wynne, Captain Farren, Captain Spark R.N., Lieutenant Colonel Clarke, Captain Sir Thomas Ross R.N., Captain Herbert R.N., Captain Hellard R.N., Major M'Kie, Captain Kennedy, Captain Ommanney R.N., Captain Gilbert R.E., Captain Broughten R.E. and Captain Labalmondiere.[53] There were also Inspectors appointed where no relief was given by the British Association, who reported to Count Strzelecki. These included:-Captain Flude B.A., Captain Dent R.N., Captain Darley R.N., Captain Haymes R.N., Brevet Major Stuart, and Brevet Major Bolton. The reason given for appointing these military personnel in places where no aid was given was stated to be "For the purpose of superintending the proceedings in execution of Orders issued under the second section of the Extension Act."

---

[53] Parliamentary Papers, Thirteenth Report of the Poor Law Commissioners 1847. Page 7.

Henry Grattan questioned the reason why so many military men were in Ireland at that time. In Parliament he said "A body of officers had been sent over to Ireland to spy out the nakedness of the land, under pretence of distributing Indian meal":[54]

His statement lends support to my suggestion that the Count Strzelecki was a spy.

Strzelecki was a Polish Count, who moved in the highest political circles in England. He had travelled extensively before coming to Ireland, and appeared to be a trusted associate of Lord Russell. When Russell was Colonial Secretary, from 1839 to 1841, Strzelecki was in Australia, where it was said that he was the first to discover gold, at Bathurst. He was advised by Governor Gipps to tell Lord Russell, but otherwise to keep it quiet, as there were too many convicts living in Australia, and the scramble for gold could not be contained. Many of the stories associated with him have been controversial, and challenged by others at the time. He went on an expedition to the interior of Australia, and named the territory Gippsland, after the Governor. A Scotsman called MacMillan claimed that he had been living there for some time and had discovered it first. This did not deter Strzelecki.

He appears to have done a geological survey of some parts of Australia, although there is a mystery about when he would have had time to do this. An English Protestant Minister, the Rev. W.B. Clarke, also claimed that he had done the same the work. Clarke wrote of Strzelecki

> You are aware that there is, in this part of the world, a foreign traveller who styles himself Count Streleski; he is a well-informed, intelligent, and active person, and a most gentlemanly, pleasant companion. His residence here, with funds at his command apparently unlimited in extent, is as great a mystery, if he be really a Polish emigrant, as he calls himself, as it was to the Americans with whom he lived, and amongst whom he journeyed, before he came hither. He may be a Pole; but I believe there is no title of Count attached to that surname in Poland; or he may be a Russian or Gallician; at any rate he was known to Captain King as Count Streleski in America; and at the dinner given in Sydney by the officers of the United States Exploring Expedition to their British friends, I heard him most affectingly (or affectedly), in a brilliant speech, discourse on the hardships of his condition. He manages, however, here to go whither he wishes, and see what he likes... [55]

Strzelecki went on many voyages on British navy ships, which suggests that he did hold some position in the British Navy. In 1837 Strzelecki sailed to Mexico on board HMS Cleopatra, whose Captain was George Grey. George Grey was the fourth son of Earl Grey, who was Prime Minister from 1830-1834. This is the man to whom Strzelecki left all his possessions, in his first will and testament. There may well be an interesting story behind this gift. This gift was later annulled.

In 1841 Strzelecki went on an expedition to Bass Strait islands on H.M.S. Beagle. The Beagle was famous as the ship on which Charles Darwin sailed around the world. The captain of the Beagle during the time in which Strzelecki sailed in it was Captain John Lort Stokes. Stokes was also a geologist, who had published articles on his geological research, and who could have helped Strzelecki with his geological explorations. In 1842, Strzelecki visited the Pacific Islands as a guest on HMS Fly.

---

[54] House of Commons Debate, *Poor Relief (Ireland)*. 26 April 1849.
[55] The Literary Gazette. London, 20 February 1841.

While he was in Australia, he and an Irish servant are reported to have climbed the highest mountain there, and to have named it after a Polish freedom fighter, Kosciuszko. Again there is some controversy over this. It is now said that he climbed the mountain next to the highest mountain.

While he was in Australia he stayed as a guest of the Governor of New South Wales, George Gipps. He then travelled to Tasmania where he was the guest of Sir John and Lady Jane Franklin, the British representatives there. Sir John Franklin was an Admiral in the Royal Navy. Strzelecki became good friends with Lady Jane Franklin. She was an amateur geologist with a fine collection of geological specimens. Perhaps she gave some of these to Strzelecki, and he used them later when he applied for membership of the Royal Geographical Society.

In 1845 Franklin led a voyage to discover the North West passage in the Arctic. His ship was lost. Many efforts were made to find the remains of the Franklin expedition. Strzelecki raised money for these further expeditions.

As a footnote to this, it is interesting that the Inuit (Eskimo) people reported seeing members of the Franklin expedition wandering across the ice starving and lost. No effort seems to have been made by the Franklin expedition to make contact with these people who could have helped them. It seems to have been a case of the colonial mind set, not making any effort to cooperate with native inhabitants of other countries, in their efforts to conquer the world.

In later years, Strzelecki travelled to Turkey. He advised Lord Russell that the Turkish ruler was not ready to give up the present Palestine. This was an enterprise which the Jewish banker Montefiore was very passionate about. Montefiore was the banker who offered to go to Ireland in January 1847, shortly before Strzelecki offered to go to Ireland, both at their own expense. The two may have cooperated together in the Irish enterprise, as well as in the enterprise to set up a Zionist homeland in Palestine.

Strzelecki was called to give evidence before a committee of enquiry of the House of Lords in 1849. He said to the committee that he stayed in Ireland during 1847 and 1848, and after the amount of aid from the British Association was used up, he continued to stay in Ireland until September 1848, doing something for the Treasury. He said

> I was as an executive officer of the British Relief Association for eighteen months, during the distress of 1847 and 1848, and afterwards, two months as an agent of the Treasury, to administer the remainder of the relief.[56]

It is a strong possibility that he was the eyes and ears of Lord Russell during the time that William Smith O'Brien and his friends were planning an insurrection in Ireland. He may be the person who advised Lord Russell to bring in a Habeas Corpus Bill as a matter of urgency. This came into force in July 1848. O Brien had been planning to wait until the autumn to hold an insurrection, but his hand was forced into acting early, or else perhaps he would have been arrested, under the Habeas Corpus Act.

As soon as O'Brien was arrested and put on trial, Strzelecki no longer was needed in the country. Henry Grattan made a point of asking in the House of Commons the names of those killed

___

[56] Parliamentary Papers 1849 (365), *Fourth report from the Select Committee of the House of Lords appointed to inquire into the operation of the Irish Poor Law,* 24th April 1849. Page Image 199 of 384 (Page number 717 in the text).

and wounded in the alleged insurrection of William Smith O'Brien. The answer was "actually none." Grattan said that his object was to show that the word "insurrection" did not actually mean "insurrection" and that there had not been an insurrection in Ireland in 1848. [57]

Perhaps Strzelecki was well disposed to Ireland. Perhaps not. On 21 November 1848, shortly after he returned from Ireland, he was awarded the Most Honourable Order of the Bath. The notes on his life say he was "One of its very first non military recipients". [58] Perhaps he was not "a non military recipient". In 1869 he was knighted by the Queen.

A book by Sir William Fraser quotes an Admiral Lyons who said

> I knew Count Strzelecki well. He was an intimate friend of Lord Palmerston, and was supposed to be employed by him in more or less secret investigations. He was a very clever, agreeable and very talkative man.

In the book there was an anecdote about the Count:-

> Count Strzelecki gave me a graphic description of the investiture of H.I.M. the Sultan with the order of the Garter: the Count attended disguised in a British Naval Uniform: he said that, as it was against the Mahometan law for the person of the Sultan to be touched, considerable embarrassment arose as to how Lord Stratford de Redcliffe could invest him: it being absolutely necessary by the Statutes of the Order that the Garter should be buckled below the left knee of every august recipient: in England this part of the ceremony being always performed by the hands of the Sovereign herself. The difficulty was increased by the fact of the Sultan wearing long robes. After severe thought, and long deliberation, it was arranged that a vertical slit should be cut in the draperies of H.I.M. through which his knee could protrude: and thus Lord Stratford was enabled to fasten on the Garter. [59]

The point of this anecdote is that Strzelecki attended disguised as a Navy Officer.

He is very often praised for going around Ireland to feed the hungry children. The reports of the Poor Law Commissioners show that he did no such thing. It was the Temporary Relieving Officers of the workhouse committees who arranged for food to be distributed in the schools. The Count stayed in his office in Sackville Street (now O'Connell Street), in Dublin, and gave his approval to the lists sent in by the Temporary Relieving Officers. This is borne out by the reports of the Relief Commissioners (Commissariat series).

A minute from Captain George F. Herbert, Commander, R.N., Inspector of Poor Laws for the Union of Donegal says "I enclose for the information of the Commissioners the list of schools in the Donegal area where the children can receive food". The Temporary Relieving Officer wrote "I am in contact with the Count Strzelecki who is in Dublin. [60]

There are inconsistencies in the reports prepared by Strzeletski which would suggest that Strzelecki was not truthful with the figures. For instance, the figures which Strzelecki gave in his

---

[57] House of Commons Debate, *Troops in Ireland.* 5 Feb 1849.

[58] http://mtkosciuszko.org.au/english/chronology.htm

[59] Sir William Fraser, *Hic and Ubique.* London 1893.

[60] Parliamentary Papers 1847-1848 (919) (955) (999), *Papers relating to proceedings for relief of distress, and state of the unions and workhouses in Ireland,* 1848. Page 59.

reports to the Poor Law Commissioners were not the same as those given by the Relieving Officers in the Reports of the Relief Commissioners. Strzelecki said that the number of children who were feed in the Donegal Union was 5635. He said that these 5635 children received 504,399 rations during the five months from 30 November 1847 to 30 April 1848.[61] Yet Captain Herbert wrote to Strzelecki on 18 January 1848 giving the number of schoolchildren attending schools in Donegal as 2,420. In this report, Captain Herbert said that it would be a great help to these school children if they could receive rations at school. This letter was written in January, so the Donegal schoolchildren could only have received rations from after that date until 30 April 1848. In another example. that of the Ballinrobe Union, Strzelecki gave the number of children fed as 11,510, and the Relieving Officer there, Dr. Dempster, gave the figure as 869 males and 741 females, 1,610 in all.[62] There are more examples of this exaggeration when one compares the reports of the two different agencies. It is clear that Strzelecki exaggerated the amount of aid which the British Association was giving to schoolchildren.

The Home Secretary Sir George Grey, (nephew of Admiral Grey), gave the same figures in Parliament as Strzelecki supplied in the Report of the Poor Law Commissioners. He said

> The returns of the first week, ending the 28th of November, showed eighteen schools, with 2,136 children daily attending them. The returns of the last week, ending the 23rd of January, showed above 44,000 children, to whom relief was afforded by 655,229 weekly rations. The increase during the intervening eight weeks was gradual. The total number of rations issued since the beginning was 2,111,513.

These figures can be shown to be untrue. They were what we would now know as "Alternative Facts". To add insult to injury, Sir George Grey used poetic language in the House of Commons to describe how much the poor Irish appreciated the aid

> They also bear testimony to the visible and daily improving condition of the poor unhappy children, to the cheering and beneficial reaction which this provision has had upon the parents, and to the faithful appropriation and distribution of the bounty by those intrusted with it.[63]

Parliament and the public were not told the truth about the administration of aid from the British Association.

There is also a mystery around the last will and testament of Count Strzelecki. It would not have become public, except that his relatives in Poland took a court action when they were disinherited. We know this because the proceedings of the Court Case were published in the Sidney Morning Herald of Monday 6 August 1877.

_____

[61] Parliamentary Papers 1847-1848 (963), *First Annual Report of the Commissioners for Administering the Laws for Relief of the Poor in Ireland.* Page 127.

[62] Parliamentary Papers 1847-1848 (919) (955) (999), *Papers relating to proceedings for relief of distress, and state of the unions and workhouses in Ireland,* 1848. (Dr. Dempster to the Commissioners Nov. 30, 1847).

[63] House of Commons Debate, *Relief of the Poor (Ireland).* 07 February 1848.

Strzelecki died on 6 October 1873. He had made a will in which he gave two sums of £1,000 each to two relations in Poland, and everything else "to his dear friend Admiral Sir George Grey". Three days before his death, he had a visit from William Ewart Gladstone, who was then Prime Minister. Gladstone advised him to change his will. Strzelecki did so, and left his money to Mr. Sawer of Le Vaux Bank. Le Vaux bank does not otherwise appear in banking literature, perhaps it was a secret bank? His relations in Poland disputed the new will. Both Gladstone, and the banker Mr. Thomson Hankey, M.P. for Peterborough and former Governor of the Bank of England, gave evidence in court that Strzelecki was of sound mind when he made his second will. They referred to the fact that he had been staying at the home of Mr. Baring shortly before his death. His Polish relations maintained that Strzelecki, the testator, "did not know and approve the contents of the later will". They lost their case. Of course they were going to lose their case if they were pitted against the power and authority of the Prime Minister of England and a former Governor of the Bank of England.

Strzelecki had also asked that all his papers would be destroyed after his death. This in itself points to the fact that he had something to hide. Distributing food through the good offices of the Workhouses may not have been the whole reason that Strzelecki was knighted by the British Queen.

Another Poor Law 1847

In 1847 Lord Russell passed a new Poor Law. It was known as the Poor Law Extension Act. Its title was "Poor Relief (Ireland). An Act to make further provision for the relief of the destitute Poor in Ireland". It was the Poor Law for Ireland "Mark 2". If the law he passed in 1837 was destructive of Irish property, and of the Irish people, this one was much worse. It gave Lord Russell the power to dispossess a large number of small Irish farmers of their land, through the Gregory clause. It gave him extra powers to dismiss Boards of Guardians of Workhouses and to appoint his own Vice Guardians. These would be paid Vice Guardians, which would add to the amount of money which would be levied on the rates. It gave him power to build more workhouses, which would cost those areas even more money. It increased the powers of the Boards of Guardians to pay for poor people to emigrate, even if they were not living in the workhouses. It also included for the first time the right of all persons to apply for relief, not only widows, children, and the infirm, but also the able bodied.

In his speeches he made many statements which misrepresented the state of things in Ireland. He put the blame for the famine, "the calamity", on the Irish landlords, for not giving employment to their tenants. He said

> The gentry and landowners have but little hold—I will not say whether it is their fault or not—they have but little hold generally on the attachment of the people. It might have been expected, as it was found, that instead of all the landowners, farmers, and labourers assembling together and devising means whereby they might meet that great calamity, there appeared great apathy on the part of the landowners, very little concern on the part of the tenants, and amongst the unfortunate people themselves who were struck by this calamity, a resignation which, in one sense, was very greatly commendable—a patient submission, which was much to be admired—but at the same time, a want of effort and exertion, which greatly aggravated that calamity under which they were suffering.[64]

He repeated the statement which he often made, of how the people in Ireland had nothing but the potato for food. Four or even five million, he claimed, were dependent on the potato. He said

> "It was the case of a people, several millions of whom—say three, four, or five millions—were dependent, not on any regular wages, not on the purchase of food, but on the growth of the potato, which they themselves cultivated, and which in this year failed to an extent, we may say, of four-fifths or five-sixths, in some places more, of the entire amount".[65]

It was a gross exaggeration to say that five millions were dependent on the potato. This can be disproved by looking at the amount of crops and animals which were produced in Ireland and exported to England during the famine. Grattan emphasised this point in the House of Commons

> "Ireland last year produced 6,000,000 quarters of grain—twice as much as was sufficient to feed the Irish people—but the Government had sent to America for bad corn to feed them, while they took the good Irish corn out of the country and brought it to London".[66]

---

[64] House of Commons Debate, *Destitute Persons (Ireland) Bill.* 31 May 1847.

[65] House of Commons Debate, *Destitute Persons (Ireland) Bill.* 31 May 1848.

[66] House of Commons Debate, *Parliament (Ireland)-Adjourned Debate.* 26 July 1848.

It was also untrue that the Irish landlord did not help his tenants. Very many of them provided work and food for their tenants when they could. However, there were many absentee landlords who did not take any responsibility for the welfare of their tenants. Lord Russell did not mention these. In another debate, Henry Grattan did draw attention to them

> there were the rents of the great absentees, which were drawn from his country and spent in this. He had a list of them, and be would give their names. There were the Duke of Devonshire and the Duke of Buckingham....Then came the Marquess of Ely and Earl Fitzwilliam, a most excellent man. There were Lords Essex, Audley, Maryborough, Middleton, Albemarle, Clifton, Ashbrook, Arden, Stafford, Lifford, Templemore, Colonel Wyndham, and Mr. Sidney Herbert. There was the Marquess of Conyngham, who said that he had not the means of improving his property. Where were all his means spent? In this country. There were the Marquess of Lansdowne, the Marquess of Anglesea, the Marquess of Donegal, and the Marquess of Bath. ...Mr. Greville, Mr. Lane Fox, and Mr. Ormsby Gore had also large properties in Ireland. He suggested that the best thing they could do would be to impose a tax of 10 per cent upon the absentee landlords.[67]

It was a question of the rich English Absentee Landlords avoiding their responsibilities and letting the poor starve. Lord Russell ignored any calls to impose a tax on absentee landlords. He continued with his justification of his new Poor Law. In his opinion, it would force the Irish landlord to give more employment on his land

> My opinion is, that this New Poor Law will induce those classes to employ a greater quantity of labour, so that those few who are left to be supported by the poor rates will be in reality destitute; and in this manner, the future improvement of Ireland may be discerned through the gloom and darkness of the present moment.[68]

Although he claimed that he introduced his new Poor Law because of the potato blight, this was merely an excuse to disguise the fact that he had a grand plan to change Ireland, and as he said "to make Ireland happy and prosperous."

In January 1847 he put into the Queen's Speech a statement about a plan for the prosperity of Ireland

> "Various Measures will be laid before you, which, if adopted by Parliament, may tend to raise the great Mass of People in Comfort, to promote Agriculture, and to lessen the Pressure of that Competition for Land which has been the fruitful Source of Crime and Misery".[69]

In 1849 he again made a statement about his grand plan for Ireland which would bring about a great social change in that country

> it is only by a total change in the state of society that these evils can be remedied; and if it is only by a total change in the state of society that these evils can be remedied, let me, with all deference to the hon. Gentleman, tell him, that if he were on those benches to-morrow to

---

[67] House of Commons Debate, *Relief of Distress (Ireland)-(Adjourned Debate)*. 12 February 1849.

[68] House of Commons Debate, *Destitute Persons (Ireland) Bill*. 31 May 1847.

[69] House of Lords Debate, *Meeting of Parliament*. 19 January 1847.

propose a measure for the purpose, that a great social change cannot be effected in one, two, or three years; that it must be the work of time; but that I do believe, with time, with patience, with a judicious adaptation of the remedies, we may arrive at that result which we all desire, that of seeing the state of Ireland improved, and at length happy.[70]

It is clear that his new Poor Law would be part of that plan for a great social change. He boasted of the fact that it was he who introduced the Poor Laws, in Ireland, one in 1837 and one in 1847

It has been my fortune to have introduced both these laws; and, had it not been for the calamity of the loss of the potato crop, I confess I should not be disposed to introduce the extended poor-law of 1847. I believe that relief in the workhouse, but for that calamity, would have been sufficient. If the Poor Law acts, as I believe it will act, beneficially, in connecting various classes in that country in one common duty... it will lay the foundation for a future condition of greater comfort and greater prosperity in that country.

The Poor Law Extension Act was passed in June 1847 and came into operation in November 1847. It made things worse.

The Gregory clause

Part of what made things worse was the" Gregory Clause" or the "Quarter Acre" clause. Sir William Gregory put forward an amendment to the Poor Law of 1847. It was that any person going to the Workhouse must occupy no more than a quarter acre of land. This person must give any more land which he occupied back to his landlord. This amendment caused immense hardship for the Irish poor. Many men died rather than give up their land.

William Gregory (1817-1892) was a Member of Parliament for Dublin from 1842-1847. He is better known to the Irish as the husband of Lady Augusta Gregory, the playwright. William Gregory became Governor of Ceylon from 1872 to 1877. He was knighted in 1885. In 1880, he married Augusta Persse. He lived in Coole, near Gort, Co. Galway. She lived on a neighbouring estate. He was 63 and she was 28 when they married. She then became Lady Gregory. She is well known to the Irish people as the co founder of the Abbey theatre in Dublin, together with William Martyn and William Butler Yeats. Ironically, one of her plays about Irish life was called "The Poor House."

William Gregory put forward the "quarter acre clause" as an amendment to the Poor Law Extension Act. It was not he who raised it first in Parliament. It was Lord Russell. Russell mentioned on 1 March 1847 that some qualification could be put into the Act so that not every destitute tenant in Ireland could claim admission to a workhouse.

if, on the other hand, we say relief is to be given to people occupying—suppose half an acre or more—there is the danger that we may be doing an injury, by perpetuating some of the worst holdings in Ireland.[71]

---

[70] House of Commons Debate, *Relief of Distress (Ireland)-(Adjourned Debate).* 12 February 1849.

[71] House of Commons Debate. *Poor Relief (Ireland) Bill.* 1 March 1847.

It was in response to the anxieties of the landlords that Lord Russell suggested a way to limit the number of people who could receive aid. He said that relief could be given only to those who had very little land, "say a half acre", he said then. William Gregory, the M.P. for Dublin, then became "his master's voice" and proposed an amendment to the Bill, which said that relief would be given only to those who held under a quarter acre of land. What he proposed was

> And be it further Enacted, That no person who shall be in the occupation, whether under lease or agreement, or as tenant-at-will, or from year to year, or in any other manner whatsoever, of any land of greater extent than the quarter of a statute acre, shall be deemed and taken to be a destitute poor person under the provisions of this Act, or of any former Act of Parliament; nor shall it be lawful for any board of guardians to grant any relief whatever in or out of the workhouse to any such occupier, his wife, or children.[72]

William Smith O'Brien objected to this clause. He said

> as he understood the Government were determined to accede to this clause, it would be useless for him to remonstrate against it. There were many instances, however, where it would operate harshly. If a man was only to have a right to out-door relief upon condition of his giving up his land, a person might receive relief for a few weeks, and become a beggar for ever. He thought this was a cruel enactment, and should therefore enter his remonstrance against it.

The Poor Law Extension Bill was passed. Just seven M.P.s voted against it. They were remembered in Ireland with gratitude. They were William Sharman Crawford, Bickham Escott, Sir De Lacy Evans, Alderman John Humphery, Alexander M'Carthy, Poulett Scrope, and William Williams. William Smith O'Brien and Herbert Curteis were tellers against the motion.[73]

The implementation of the Gregory clause made matters worse for those without work or money. As soon as people gave up their land to their landlord, their homes were knocked down. They then had no home to come back to.

The landlords were very opposed to the new Poor Law extension Act. They protested that "able bodied" men would be supported in the workhouse in idleness. These men would be paid to do nothing. Landlords tried to think of other ways to ease the increase in rates which this would impose on them. Their only choice seemed to be to evict their tenants and knock down their houses.

Lord Russell knew that his new Poor Law would accelerate this move to evict the poor and to change the overall occupation of land. Once the poor were cleared off the land, larger farms would become available for new owners. This plan was already a topic which had been considered before the famine. Russell referred to his plans in a speech which he made to the House of Commons in March 1847. He said his plans would be a "vast transition of great difficulty and accompanied by great distress", but that it was necessary for the future development of Ireland.

The question of how to clear poor tenants off the land had been one of the items which the Devon Commission had examined in 1845. The heading in the Devon Report was "consolidation of

---

[72] House of Commons Debate, *Poor Relief (Ireland) Bill*. 29 March 1847.

[73] House of Commons Debate, *Poor Relief (Ireland) Bill*. 29 March 1847.

farms: different modes of effecting, and comments upon them." This Commission had been set up by Sir Robert Peel. It provided a great deal of background information on the number of people who were dependent on the land, and the size of farms of the majority of the population. The idea of land clearances was already in the air. The effect of the policies of Lord Russell in his new Poor Law was to cause the evictions of hundreds of poor tenants. This could create the opportunity for a new class of landowner to move in. In particular, his policies did prepare the ground for land clearances to take place in Connaught.

Lord Russell's new Poor Law of 1847 did not "raise the great mass of people in comfort." In particular, the Gregory clause added to the distress in Ireland. It caused many of the poor to be evicted. It increased the numbers in the workhouses. It added to the amount which had to be paid in the rates. It also caused the landlords to think of paying for their tenants to go to another country.

Guardians dismissed and paid vice guardians appointed.

Another provision in the new Poor Law gave Lord Russell and the Poor Law Commissioners the power to remove elected Boards of Guardians, and replace them with paid Vice Guardians. This they started to do immediately after the Act was passed. The Boards they removed were in the poorest areas. These were the areas where it was hardest to collect the rates. The Vice Guardians were sent in to enforce that collection. Many of these paid Vice Guardians were army personnel.

Irish M.P.s objected to these Vice Guardians. Fitzstephen French complained that they were causing ruin and demoralisation where they were sent in

> In thirty-five unions the Commissioners dismissed the guardians, and sent their paid officers to undertake the management, who were rapidly involving them in ruin and demoralisation, Out of nineteen unions in Connaught, fifteen had their elected guardians dismissed.[74]

The Earl Fitzwilliam expressed his distrust of the powers given to the paid Vice Guardians

> shocked at the idea of those vice-guardians, having no connexion with the country, but sent down from Dublin by the Poor Law Commissioners, being empowered to determine the amount of rate, and to levy the rate, and, in default of payment of the rate, to distrain the person that ought to pay the rate. That was as unconstitutional on a small scale as it would be unconstitutional on a large scale to give money without the will of Parliament.[75]

The main reason for the appointment of the new paid vice guardians was to collect the rates. Yet this was an impossible task. These were Unions where the farms were small, where the land was unproductive, and no rates could be levied. The conditions in these workhouses were terrible. The Boards of Guardians could not pay for food and fuel for all the poor who had come there. One such Union was Carrick on Shannon, where the guardians wrote that had no money to provide coffins for those who died. An entry in their minute book said

> The applicants for admission were so numerous they were not entered in the Application and

---

[74] House of Commons Debate, *Poor Laws (Ireland)-Rate in Aid Bill-Adjourned (Third Night)*, 02 April 1849.

[75] House of Lords Debate, Poor Laws (Ireland)-Rate in Aid Bill. 18 May 1849.

Report Book but were upwards of 600 persons looking for relief.[76]

The same Workhouse reported that they had to bury the dead without coffins. In another case, that of the workhouse in Castlebar, the bailiffs came and seized the blankets and even the straw to pay for the debts of the workhouse. A question was asked in the House of Commons about the fact that all the furniture had been seized by the sheriff. Mr. Bourke inquired of the right hon. Gentleman the Secretary for Ireland

> "whether it be true that a sheriff's sale of all the furniture and clothing has taken place in the workhouse of Castlebar; and what provision has been made by the vice-guardians for the support of the poor of that union since the period of said sale?"

Sir W. Somerville admitted that all the effects and furniture of the workhouse had been sold.

> The difficulty in obtaining payment of rates led to this catastrophe. He was happy, however, to be able to add, that the vice-guardians had made such arrangements as enabled them to retain the paupers in the house.[77]

The Vice Guardians were accused of spending money extravagantly where they were in charge. Mr. Napier, MP for Dublin University, complained of the luxury items which were purchased by the vice guardians

> With regard to what were called the bankrupt unions, he had two advertisements which would show to the House the manner in which the affairs there were conducted. The advertisement requested tenders to be sent in— For the best port wine,—per dozen; the best sherry wine,—per dozen; the best arrowroot,—per lb.; the best mustard,—per lb.; the best tea,—per lb.; the best lump sugar,—per cwt.; the best XX porter,—per dozen; the best whisky,—per gallon; the best sweet oil,—per gallon; the best mould candles,—per dozen lbs.; the best white bread,—per 41b. loaf. These were the cases of unions under the management of vice-guardians, and subject to the control of the Poor Law Commissioners. Was it fair or just that the inhabitants of unions, who had to support their own poor, should, in addition to these charges, be compelled to pay for the support of such unions as those he had referred to?[78]

It is interesting that it was in the areas where the Vice Guardians were in charge that most of the money collected by the British Association was spent. £196,521 was spent in these Unions, and just £3,190 in four other Distressed Unions. Fitzstephen French said

> The grants from Government and the British Association were, to the four undissolved unions, but three thousand one hundred and ninety pounds; whilst to the fourteen dissolved ones, they amounted to one hundred and ninety-six thousand five hundred and twenty-one

---

[76] Minute Book of the Board of Guardians of Carrick on Shannon Workhouse for 1847. Leitrim Public Library, Ballinamore, Co. Leitrim.

[77] House of Commons Debate, *Workhouse of Castlebar.* 25 May 1848.

[78] House of Lords Debate, *Poor Relief (Ireland) Bill.* 16 July 1849.

pounds[79].

The imposition of the rule of the paid Vice Guardians made matters worse in the "Distressed districts."

The Vice Guardians did raise more money for rates in these so called "Distressed Unions." A return was made to the Houses of Parliament of the amount of debt which had been in the Distressed Unions when the Vice Guardians were in control, and the amount of debt which these Unions had when the Vice Guardians were relieved of their duties. They had raised a large amount of rates in these poor areas. Yet in all cases the Vice Guardians had left their Unions with a larger debt than when they took over.[80]

This experiment with the vice guardians only lasted a year. In 1849 their contracts were not renewed, and elected Guardians were once again put in charge of the workhouses.

The march to Delphi and our red brethren of the Choctau nation.

One of the Unions in which the elected guardians were removed and vice guardians were appointed was the Westport Union in County Mayo. The events leading to the removal of the Board of Guardians have been commemorated in recent years by an annual walk across the mountains to a hunting lodge in Delphi in Mayo. In 1847, hundreds of people were starving, and they decided to walk to Delphi Lodge to ask for help. They were refused help at the lodge and had to return home in a worse state than when they set out. The background to this is the refusal of the Poor Law Commissioners to help the workhouses in the poorest parts of the country.

The minute books for the Westport Union are in the National Library of Ireland.[81] The minutes for 1847 show that very little money in rates could be collected in the Westport and Louisburg areas. The record showed that one landlord in particular, The Earl of Lucan, refused to pay any rates. Lucan was accused by the M.P. Poulett Scrope in the House of Commons of not paying his poor rates for the workhouse. He strongly denied that this was true. The records of the Westport Workhouse show differently.

The chairman of the Board of Guardians was the Marquess of Sligo. From January 1847 to March 1847 the Marquess and some of the other guardians paid all the expenses for food and fuel for the Westport Union out of their own pockets. He and the Guardians wrote frequently to the Poor Law Commissioners in Dublin, asking for help. They received nothing. In April 1847 the Marquess of Sligo decided that they would pay no more. The Guardians took the decision to close down the workhouse and to send all the poor people away. The minutes of the Westport Workhouse for 24 April 1847 read "Number in Workhouse, Nil". There were no inmates. There had been 540 in the workhouse in the previous weeks. The people who were put out of the workhouse had nowhere to go. They decided to walk to the hunting lodge of the Marquess of Sligo, Delphi Lodge, in the mountains, ten miles from Louisburg. At the lodge they were refused help. The poor people had to walk back over the mountain

---

[79] House of Commons Debate, *Poor Laws (Ireland)-Rate in Aid Bill-Adjourned Debate (Third Night)*. 02 April 1849.

[80] Parliamentary Papers, 1850 (251), *Poor Law Unions Ireland. Return showing the financial return of each Union in Ireland, where paid guardians were appointed.*

[81] Westport Poor Law Union Minutes Books, MSS 12,607 – 12,612. National Library of Ireland Manuscript Section.

to Louisburg. Some of them died on the way. This is the story which inspired the annual walk to Delphi to commemorate the famine. It is overlooked that the background to this tragedy was the failure of the Poor Laws and the Poor Law Commissioners in Dublin to provide for the Irish poor.

When the Guardians of the Westport workhouse took the radical step of closing down the workhouse, it caused the Poor Law Commissioners to advance £50 so that it could be opened again. The following week showed that there were again 500 people in the Westport Workhouse. The actions of the Marquess of Sligo and the other guardians can be understood. The Poor Law Commissioners would have happily let them go on paying for the expenses of the workhouse forever.

The Choctau Indians have joined in this Famine walk to Delphi. They have been praised for having collected 170 dollars for the starving Irish in 1847. Their contribution was acknowledged in the House of Commons on 20 July 1847. Mr. Brotherton the M.P. for Salford read an account of contributions from America.

> New York, May 19.
> Out of one contribution of 170 dollars, the largest part was contributed by the children of the forest, our red brethren of the Choctau nation. Even these distant men (as the chairman of the New York committee well observes) have felt the force of Christian sympathy and benevolence, and have given their cheerful aid in this good cause, though they are separated from you by so many miles of land and an ocean's breadth.[82]

This money was given to the British Ambassador in Washington, Sir Richard Pakenham. He duly transferred it to the Foreign Office from where it went into the funds of the British Association. Lord Palmerston wrote a reply thanking the American people for their generosity to the Irish, and sent it to Sir Richard Pakenham to give to the American Government.

The Choctau Indians had their own "trail of tears" in 1830, when the British made a deal with them to take over their lands in Oklahoma, and to relocate them on a reservation near Washington. Many of them died on the long march to their new settlement. Their march to Delphi recognises the common suffering of these two peoples, the Irish and the native American.

Two paid vice guardians were appointed to run the workhouse in Westport. These were William Robert Lecky and Arthur Thomas. They pursued the collection of the Poor Rates with vigour. At the time they were appointed, there was £8,420 outstanding in uncollected rates. With the help of the army they collected £13,220 in 1848-1849. This put the Union under even more strain.

This march to Delphi is a small vignette of the disastrous effect of setting up these workhouses, and how little Lord Russell cared about whether his policies caused the deaths of the poor or not. It can only be surmised that as far as he was concerned, incidents like this advanced his policy of land clearance, so that he could finally "lay the foundation for a future condition of greater comfort and greater prosperity in that country".

---

[82] House of Commons Debate, *Donation from the United States*. 20 July 1847.

Emigration

The Irish were the refugees and boat people of the 1840's.

There was mass emigration of the Irish 1847, because of the New Poor Law of Lord Russell. The new law frightened the landlords and made them believe that they would have to pay greatly increased rates, because for the first time, able bodied destitute poor would be admitted to the workhouses. The landlords started to think of ways to reduce this cost. The best plan they could think of would be to export their poor tenants to another country. Emigration would cost them a once off sum of £5 a head. The support of those people in a workhouse would cost them £5 each year for the lifetime of the pauper. Some of the landlords decided to charter ships and send their poor to Canada.

The ships they chartered were often referred to as coffin ships. In 1847, 97,953 people went on these ships to Gros Isle in Canada. Of that number, 8,671 died, through fever or drowning. A return of these numbers is given in the Parliamentary Papers relative to Emigration to the British Provinces in North America in 1847.[83]

Many of the ships which came to Gros Isle came from ports in Ireland. Some also came from ports in England, such as Liverpool or Greenock and some from Bremen in Germany. The majority of the deaths were on those ships which came from Irish ports or from Liverpool.

One of the most notorious of the landlords who sent his tenants to Canada was Lord Palmerston. He was at that time Foreign Minister in the government of Lord Russell. He would have known well in advance about the provisions of the new Poor Law, and would have made an early decision to move people off his estates in Sligo. A thousand people were shipped off from his estates. The first ship which was sent out by his agents, the "Carricks" sank off the coast of Newfoundland, and almost all were drowned. This was in April 1847.

Lord Palmerston denied in Parliament that he had any knowledge of the poor conditions that his tenants were in when they sailed on these ships. He said that it was his agents, Stewart and Kincaid, who was responsible for this. However there is in existence a letter dated 23 March 1847 from Kincaid, saying

On the authority of your Lordship when in London last Christmas I have already chartered two vessels.[84]

It is a fact that his agent continued to send tenants on ships to Gros Isle, until November 1847. It would seem that Palmerston was lying. In particular, he must have been aware of a report which was sent from the Governor of Canada, Lord Elgin, to the Colonial secretary, Lord Grey. The report

---

[83] Parliamentary Papers,1847-48 (932) (964) (971) (985). Emigration. Papers relative to emigration to the British provinces in North America. (in continuation of the papers presented December 1847) *A page is reproduced in the Appendices.*

[84] Desmond Norton. https://www.ucd.ie/economics/research/workingpapers/2001/WP01.19.pdf. page 8. The quotation is "Note also that Palmerston's decision to initiate large-scale assisted emigration was apparently made in December 1846. Thus, Kincaid's letter to Palmerston dated 23 March 1847 informed: On the authority of your Lordship when in London last Christmas I have already chartered two vessels." Kincaid letter 13 BR 146/9/3.

included a letter from one of the legislators of the Emigration laws in Quebec, Mr. William Adair, which gave a damning report of the conduct of Lord Palmerston

> For instance, there have been this year about 1,000 persons shipped off by the agents of Lord Palmerston, who not only promised them clothes, but they were assured that his Lordship had agents at Quebec, to whom instructions had been sent to pay them all from 2L to 5L each family, according to their numbers. On their arrival, however, no agents of his Lordship were to be found, and they were then thrown upon the bounty of the Government here, and the charitable donations of private individuals. If his Lordship was aware of this most horrible and heartless conduct on the part of his Irish agents, and he one of the Ministers of the Crown, I dare not say what he would deserve. But that charity, my Lord, which "thinketh no evil," would teach me to hope that a nobleman of England, high in the confidence of Her Most Gracious Majesty, and sharing in the honourable administrations of her Government, could not so far forget that duty which he owed to God, his Sovereign, and his country, but that it was a wanton and unauthorised act of worthless and unprincipled hirelings, in whose bosoms every principle of humanity and every germ of mercy had become totally extinct.[85]

Every germ of mercy was evidently totally extinct in the bosom of Lord Palmerston in trying to avoid the expenses of the new Poor Law Extension Act for Ireland.

Lord Palmerston's castle in Ireland was at Classiebawn, Co. Sligo. His home became famous in 1979, when the IRA exploded a bomb which killed Lord Mountbatten, who was staying there. Lord Mountbatten was married to Edwina Ashley, of the family of Lord Palmerston.

Many other landlords in the west of Ireland also shipped their poor tenants out of the country. The problem with this mass clearance was that the landlords were creating enemies for themselves amongst the people who were being forced to emigrate. Some of these landlords were murdered by their tenants.

One of these was Major Mahon of the Pakenham Mahon family in Strokestown in Co. Roscommon. His brother explained to him that it would be much cheaper to send his tenants to America than to support them in the workhouse at home. He made the decision to send some 300 people out to Gros Isle in Canada. A third died of fever on the way and more died in Gros Isle when they landed. Major Mahon was shot on his way home from a meeting of the Board of Guardians of the Roscommon workhouse, evidently by a relation of some of those who had died. A report from the Roscommon and Leitrim Gazette newspaper gave an account of the event.

> It becomes our painful duty to confirm the report of the death of the above lamented gentleman. It appears that Major Mahon was returning home from Roscommon, after attending a meeting of the Guardians of that union;- he travelled in an open Phaeton, accompanied by Dr. Shanley, and his servant, who sat behind, and had proceeded within 4 miles of his residence, when he received the fatal shot.- The particulars of which appear more fully in the following depositions at the Inquest, which was held before T.P.Peyton, Esq., Coroner:-Terence Shanley, Surgeon of Strokestown, deposed that on Tuesday, the 2nd of November, he was returning from Roscommon with the deceased Major Mahon, in his phaeton, and when they had nearly reached the bridge of Doorty, county of Roscommon, a

---

[85] Parliamentary Papers, 1847-48 (932) (964) (971) (985). Emigration. Papers relative to emigration to the British provinces in North America. (in continuation of the papers presented December 1847). Page image 40 of 154.

shot was fired from the right side of the road, the greater part of the contents lodged in the side and breast of the late Major Denis Mahon, 1 of the slugs or balls lodged in the arm of the deponent,; the deceased immediately dropped the reins and leaned back-his hat fell off-the deceased never spoke afterwards,-deponent has no doubt but the death of the deceased was caused by the gunshot wound and the internal haemorrhage consequent thereon. – Deponent laid hold of the reins as soon as possible after the shot was fired; looked around and saw in the fields a man with a gun in his hand, and pointed towards them; the man attempted to fire, but the gun burned priming; it was dark, and cannot accurately describe the size or description of the man, but from the light caused by the flash of the pan, he saw it was a cap the man had on.- Deponent immediately after saw a man in the act of passing them on the road with a gun, who, he believed to be the assassin that fired the fatal shot.[86]

There was a debate in the House of Commons in December 1847 about this shooting. The accusation was made that the priest had made a sermon at mass urging the killing of Major Mahon. John O Connell M.P read into the record of Parliament the denial of the priest, Fr. Michael MacDermott, P.P., Strokestown.

The cruelties exercised against a tenantry whose feelings were already wound up to woeful and vengeful exasperation by the loss of their exiled relatives, as well as by hunger and pestilence, which swept so many victims into an untimely grave—in my opinion, may be assigned as the sole exciting cause of the disastrous event which has occurred. I saw no necessity for the idle display of a large force of military and police surrounding the poor man's cabin, setting fire to the roof, while the half-starved, half-naked children were hastening away from the flames with yells of despair, while the mother lay prostrate on the threshold writhing in agony, and the heartbroken father remained supplicating on his knees. I saw no need for this demonstration of physical force; nor did I see any need for brutal triumph and exultation when returning after these feats were nobly performed. Nor can I conceive that the feelings of humanity should permit any man to send his bailiffs to revisit those scenes of horror and conflagration, with an order, if they found a hut built or a fire lighted in the murky ruins, to demolish the one and extinguish the other, thus leaving the wretched outcasts no alternative but to perish in a ditch. In my opinion, these scenes, of which I can only draw a very inefficient portrait, had more to do with the murder of Major Mahon than all the thundering denunciations of the Vatican could effect, had they been rolled on his head. [87]

Apart from those who were sent on coffin ships to North America, those who could raise the money left Ireland and went to the place they knew best, to England. It was quite easy for the able bodied Irish to get to England. From most inland counties it was possible to walk to the ports of Dublin, Sligo, Cork or Drogheda. The fare was just 2 shillings and 6 pence on the deck of a ship to Liverpool. It was reported in the House of Lords that 150,000 came to the port of Liverpool between January 1847 and July 1847. Liverpool could not support this number of poor people.

In mid January 1847 the Lord Mayor and the politicians of Liverpool pleaded with Lord Russell to give them some assistance to feed the Irish who had arrived in their city. By 21 January, 1,900 Irish had arrived, and were coming to the workhouses looking for food. Some of them arrived in a state of

[86] Roscommon and Leitrim Gazette. *Assassination of Major Mahon-Inquest.* Saturday November 6, 1847.
[87] House of Commons Debate, *Crime and Outrage (Ireland).* 13 December 1847.

fever, and the people of Liverpool were frightened. Large ships were put into the docks, and the people who were sick were confined there. It was said that people in Liverpool collected money to pay the fares to London of the Irish who landed in their port. The Home Secretary responded to the Mayor of Liverpool by saying that they had no money to give to them.

What the government did then was to change the law. There had been a law that a person must have been born in the area in which he asked for relief, or otherwise he was not entitled to receive it. This was known as the law of settlement. The government revived this law, so that the Irish would not be entitled to receive relief in the towns of England. Many Irish were shipped back to Dublin, where they became a burden on the Dublin workhouses.

Some of the Irish who came to Liverpool had the means to sail to America. It was reported in the House of Commons that at least 120,000 continued to New York and New Orleans in the first six months of 1847. Those people at least were independent, and made their own choice to leave Ireland.

The Poor Law Extension Act gave additional permission to Boards of Guardians to pay the fares of those who were destitute, to emigrate, even if they were not inmates of the workhouses. At least a few thousand were helped in this way.

There was another scheme of emigration which was organised by the workhouses. It was the scheme to send orphan girls between the ages of 14 and 18 to Australia. The government of Australia decided to use some of the money which they had received from selling land in Australia, to import women to the colony. There were at that time seven men for every woman living there. 4,000 young girls from Irish workhouses, and 10,000 girls from English workhouses had their passages paid to Australia, between 1848 and 1850. Their lives are well documented in the records of Australia. There is a Museum in Sydney, Hyde Park Barracks Museum, which commemorates the lives of 4114 young Irish girls who arrived there from workhouses in Ireland between 1848 and 1850.

The process of emigration from Ireland was supported by the Poor Law extension Act of 1847. This emigration continued throughout the nineteenth century, as Irish emigrants sent home the money for their relations to emigrate also. The population of Ireland declined at an alarming rate. In 1841 the census returns showed that the population of Ireland was 8,100,000. In 1851 it was 6,500,000. In 1901 it was 4,000,000. In 1951 it was 2,900,000. This emigration changed the composition of Irish society for generations. It was the young and able bodied who left. Those who remained were grandparents and grandchildren.

Grattan said in Parliament that he never heard that you could improve the lot of a country by sending all its young people away, and leaving only the very young and the very old. This is what happened in Ireland, as a result of the policies of Lord Russell.

More Workhouses Built

The Poor Law Extension Act of 1847 gave Lord Russell the power to build more workhouses. This was one of the programmes which he set in motion in 1848. He set up a Boundary Commission to establish where these new workhouses should be built. Lord Russell spoke in the House of Commons about the Boundary Commission in a speech on Relief of Distress in Ireland in April 1849

> The Government had appointed a commission for the purpose of arranging the boundaries, and at its head was Captain Larcombe, as intelligent an individual as the Government could select. He (Lord J. Russell) had repeatedly seen Captain Larcombe since this subject came under consideration, who had now returned to Ireland for the purpose of carrying out the recommendations of the commission, and would draw up a paper stating what new unions he thought it absolutely necessary to make.[88]

Lord Russell gave a justification for sub-dividing the Unions.

> if many of the unions had been smaller, and many of the electoral divisions been of less considerable acreage and population, it would have conduced better, he admitted, to the working of the poor-law.

He was suggesting that the awful loss of life would not have happened if the Unions had been smaller and there had been more workhouses. This does not follow at all. What the people needed was food, as Daniel O Connell had asked for. They did not need more workhouses.

The Boundary Commission made a number of recommendations over the next two years. They said that 50 new workhouses should be built. These were mainly in the poorer areas in the west of Ireland. The Unions in these areas were to be sub-divided and a new workhouse built in each new Union. This meant that these poor Unions had to provide the money from their rate payers to pay for yet another workhouse. It imposed a severe burden on these western Unions that were already in difficulties. It is hard to know whether this policy was designed by Lord Russell to crush the landlords in these areas totally.

The ratepayers of Ireland were very opposed to these new workhouses. The Anglo Celt published an editorial about the proposed dismemberment of the Cavan Union

> The areas of both Unions seem to us far too small to support workhouses, with their expensive train of officers. The new workhouses will increase the burden of rates on our people. [89]

The workhouses which existed in the west of Ireland were unable to support themselves. Rates could not be collected to pay for their upkeep. It was obvious that these Unions could not afford to pay for more workhouse buildings and also for the staff to run them. Fitzstephen French gave an account of a description of a workhouse in the West of Ireland which a journalist described in the Spectator magazine

---

[88] House of Commons Debate, Poor Relief (Ireland). 26 April 1849.

[89] Anglo Celt, Cavan. May 31 1850.

I saw many of the sick, including dysentery patients, three in a bed. The mortality, I was told after, amounted to forty in the week. In the wards for idiots and for orphan children (many of the latter being apparently not more than two or three years old), there was neither nurse nor fire-screen; but the latter was scarcely needed, as the handful of smouldering turf-embers, around which the inmates of the wards crouched, was insufficient to inflict any material injury upon them. The dormitories for paupers not in the sick wards or sheds presented a strange appearance—in none of them was there a semblance of a bedstead. They consisted of galleries divided longitudinally by two partitions of wood open at the top, and leaving a passage between them end to end. In each of the long narrow apartments thus formed, there was a raised ledge or stairs upon either side, about five inches high, and extending the whole length upon which the paupers sleep promiscuously like dogs in a kennel; a quantity of bed-clothes lay upon those ledges folded up, and these, as well as the floor and walls, were much cleaner than might be expected. [90]

The cost of building the first 131 workhouses was £1,200,000 sterling, and this had put a huge strain on the Irish landowners. Russell now proposed to increase that burden by building a further fifty workhouses.

The architect George Wilkinson drew up a new design for the second phase of workhouses. The new design did not have the decorative elements of the earlier workhouses, which were described as Elizabethian. The earlier buildings had some of the decorative motifs of the Gothic Revival, such as pointed arches, gable windows and multiple high chimney stacks. In the second phase Wilkinson used the severity and restraint of the Greek Revival style which had become popular for public buildings. There were very few decorative elements in the new workhouses. There was one decorative feature in the plans for the new phase of workhouses which was rather chilling. It was the entrance gate in the centre of the two front blocks. It was known as a Lych Gate. A lych gate was a feature of medieval churchyards. In the middle ages corpses were buried in a winding cloth, without a coffin. The corpse was often kept in the shelter of a Lych gate before burial. The word lych was an old English word for a corpse. It was an ominous feature to put at the centre of a workhouse. It suggested that those who entered were about to die.[91]

There were other changes in the plans for the second phase of workhouse building. The main change was that two large blocks were added to the front of the buildings, to accommodate children. So many people had died from starvation and fever that there was now a need to accommodate orphans on their own. Wilkinson also designed alterations for the older workhouses, so that two front blocks for children could be added on to them. These blocks were to house children from 2 years to 16 years of age. It is because of these blocks for children that the phrase "workhouse howl" has been recorded, to recall the sounds from the children's blocks as they were going to sleep at night.[92] It is possible that many of these children were not orphans, and that their parents put them in the workhouses while they emigrated to find work. The number of children in the workhouses increased

---

[90] House of Commons Debate, *Poor Laws (Ireland)- Rate in Aid Bill.* 26 March 1849. vol 103 cc1327
[91] This name for the central gate of the workhouse is the name which is used locally in Bawnboy. It has also been suggested that the inspiration for the gate could have been the French Porte Clochere.
[92] A resident of Bawnboy remembers her father praying for the children in the workhouse and telling her that as a child he could hear them howling at night.

between 1847 and 1852, and then gradually decreased. In 1847 there were 51,514 children in the workhouses in Ireland out of a total of 104,200 inmates.[93] In May 1852 there were 83,757 children out of a total of 186,879 inmates. In April 1853 the number had dropped to 62,695 out of a total of 146,141 inmates.[94] From then on the numbers started to reduce and the workhouses were never really full. In later years some parents came back for their children when they could afford to. The list of people who were assisted to emigrate from workhouses shows also that many children were supported to join their families in America or Australia.

In the end, just thirty workhouses were built in the second phase, and not the fifty, first envisaged by Lord Russell. The thirty new workhouses were ready for occupation by 1853. The only one built in Ulster was in Bawnboy, in Co. Cavan. The new workhouses were never full, and did not justify their building. The census returns of 1911 shows that there were only 57 people in Bawnboy workhouse at that time. (It was listed in the census as being in the townsland of Corrasmongan, in Bawnboy, Co. Cavan.) Most of these were blind or decrepit and the others were small children. At that time it was really serving as part old peoples' home, and part orphanage.

The building of the workhouses in Ireland was never justifiable, but the second phase of building workhouses was indefensible. It led to an increase in the burden of rates in the Unions least able to pay for them.

---

[93] Parliamentary Papers, Summary of the weekly returns of First Report of Poor Law Commissioners 1847-48. *Paupers in the union workhouses in Ireland, from the 4th of April 1846 to 10th of April 1847. This page is reproduced in the Appendices.*

[94] Parliamentary Papers, 1852-53 (1645), *Sixth Annual Report of the Commissioners for administering the Laws for the Relief of the Poor in Ireland.* (Page Image 10 of 169).

The Pope in Rome and Revolution in Ireland

There had been revolutions throughout Europe in 1848. Lord Russell and Lord Palmerston were very concerned that the Irish would revolt, and they devised a plan to stop this. The plan involved asking the Pope, Pope Pius the ninth (Pio Nono), to direct the Irish bishops and priests to forbid their parishioners to rebel. Lord Russell offered to the Pope that he would build new churches in Ireland, and pay a salary to the Catholic priests, as part of this negotiation.

The Pope was at that time dependent for help on England. There was a Republican revolt in Italy, and the existence of the Papal States was threatened. In 1848 the Pope was held under siege by a mob and confined to the Vatican. At one point the Pope asked both England and Poland if he might have asylum in one of their countries if he had to leave Italy. The head of his government, Pellegrino Rossi, was assassinated on 15 November 1848 and the Pope left the Vatican and did not return until April 1850. It was rumoured that Pietro Sterbini, the leader of the Republican group in Italy, instigated the murder.

Lord Russell sent the Earl of Minto on a "semi diplomatic mission" to the Pope, in November 1847. The Earl of Minto asked the Pope to issue an edict to his priests in Ireland "in defence of agitation."[95] (In a note to Lord Palmerston, the Earl of Minto said that he gave the Pope some translations of articles which had appeared in Irish papers, of speeches made by Irish priests.)

The Earl of Minto was the father-in-law of Lord Russell. Russell had married Frances Elliot-Murray-Kynynmound, the daughter of the Earl of Minto, in 1841. The Earl was working closely with Lord Russell while he was in Rome. In December 1847, questions were asked in the House of Commons about what precisely the Earl of Minto was doing in Rome? Lord Palmerston said

> Lord Minto is not at Rome in any official capacity; he has no power and no instructions to negotiate any convention whatever with the Court of Rome…[96]

It would seem that Palmerston was being economic with the truth.

In 1848, Russell and Lord Palmerston continued to put pressure on the Pope to accept a salary for the clergy. Palmerston wrote a letter for transmission to the Pope and sent it to Lord Russell for his approval. He wrote "I have prepared a translation in Italian as I understand his Holiness does not speak English". The letter began

> Downing Street October 27 1848
> The Queen's Government have under their consideration a proposition for making a provision by law for the Roman Catholic Clergy of Ireland, such provisions to include stipends to the bishops and clergy, and adequate sums for the repair and maintenance of places of worship.[97]

---

[95] George Fitz-Hardinge Berkeley, Joan Weld Berkeley, *Italy in the Making: June 1846 to 1 January 1848, Volume 2.* Cambridge. Three volumes from 1932 to 1940.

[96] House of Commons Debate, *Diplomatic Relations with Rome.* 10 December 1847.

[97] Public Record Office, Kew. PRO 30/22/7D/58. Folios 176-9: J.R. memorandum to the Pope on Irish R.C. Clergy, 1848, Oct.27, Downing Street.

Russell was accused in Parliament of trying "to rule Ireland through Rome." He and Peel certainly went out of their way to improve the lot of the clergy in Ireland. In 1845, Sir Robert Peel increased the grant of money to the Catholic Seminary in Maynooth, Co. Kildare, to £26,000 a year. He also gave £30,000 for new buildings there. These were designed by Augustus Pugin. (Pugin was the architect who worked with Charles Barry on the new Houses of Parliament in London, which were being built at the same time.) Pugin designed the picturesque St. Mary's Square, in the centre of Maynooth College. It is a distinguishing feature of the college. The new buildings were erected between 1845 and 1850.

The additional grant to Maynooth College made it possible for the Bishops of Ireland to increase to 500 the number of young men who would train for the priesthood there. In 1847 there was an inspection of the institution of Maynooth by a committee of the Houses of Parliament. This report showed details of the courses which were followed by the seminarians. They included studies in Logic, Metaphysics, Ethics, French, Latin, Greek, Hebrew, Irish and Elocution. The students spent eight years at their studies. The young men were treated well. The diet included boiled mutton and beef, and beer for dinner. The senior students received £20 each year towards their expenses. The lecturers were well paid. The salaries ranged from £130 to £30 a year. The one proviso which the government laid down was that all students must swear an oath of allegiance to the Crown.[98]

The investment of the government in Maynooth and in other seminaries throughout Ireland was a significant factor in the development of Irish society. Thousands of young Irish men and women attended these seminaries and were fervent in their defence of the Catholic faith. They were well educated and became leaders in their communities. Their values were very conservative, and this influenced the people in their congregations. Irish society became more and more conservative as the years went by. The most prized achievement for an Irish mother was to have a priest in the family. For the average Irishman, allegiance to the Church in Rome was a very strong part of his identity. His Catholic faith also included an element of rebellion against the Protestant ruling class. Unfortunately the Irishman was not aware that his illusion of independence had been brought about by the policies of Peel and Russell. The Bishops of Ireland accepted the funds to develop Maynooth. They were, after all, more interested in the spiritual development of their flock, than in their existence in this life. The bishops refused the offer of salaries for the clergy. It might have created the wrong impression amongst the laity if the priests were paid by the government in England. However it is certain that the priests did their best to dissuade the people from open revolt. This is what Peel and Russell had in mind. They had prepared the ground against any revolt from the majority of the Irish population.

The year of 1848 which saw so many revolutions across Europe was known as the "Springtime of the Peoples." There were revolts in Vienna, Budapest and Prague. In France, Louis Phillipe, the Citizen King, was overthrown in February 1848. Louis Phillipe was of the House of Orleans, and a cousin of King Louis XVI. Louis XVI was sent to the guillotine on 21 January 1793, during the French Revolution. In 1830, Louis Phillipe managed to be elected as a "citizen king" of France. In 1848, the

---

[98] Parliamentary Papers, 1847-1848 (890). Second Report of the visitors of Maynooth College 1847. Page 6 of 8.

people revolted against his rule, and declared a Republic. Lord Russell and Lord Palmerston had every reason to be afraid of a revolt in Ireland.

Daniel O Connell was more aware of the strategies of Lord Russell than most. He may have realised how Lord Russell and the Earl of Minto could influence the Pope. There was certainly a reason why he decided to go to see the Pope in 1847. He had become disillusioned with the policies of Lord Russell. He made a last sad speech in the House of Commons in February 1847 where he said

> He had not said one word to produce irritation—he had not uttered one word of reproach—and without doing so, he called upon Parliament to appoint Commissioners to make inquiries in all parts of Ireland into the circumstances of those who were able to give—to specify and to name them, and to assess them for so much as they ought to contribute. He was afraid the House was not sufficiently aware of the extent of the misery; he did not think the Members were sufficiently impressed with the horrors of the situation of the people of Ireland; he did not think they understood the miseries—the accumulation of miseries—under which the people were at present suffering. It had been estimated that 5,000 adults and 10,000 children had already perished from famine; and that 25 per cent of the whole population would perish unless the House should afford effective relief. They would perish of famine and disease unless the House did something speedy…[99]

Then O'Connell set out on a journey to see the Pope. He clearly wished to meet with the Pope personally and to explain to him the situation of Irish people. O'Connell did not get as far as Rome. He died in Genoa on 15 May 1847, at the age of 71. His last wishes included sending his heart to Rome, and his body to Ireland. It is doubtful if he could have influenced the Pope to change his attitude towards Ireland. We will never know.

The son of Daniel O' Connell, John O'Connell, made a strange accusation in Parliament about the assassination of the Pope's Foreign Minister

> the secret mission of Lord Minto was not yet forgotten. If the tree might be judged by its fruits, it yet remained to be proved that the sad occurrences in Rome, the assassinations, outrages, and violence that reigned there now, had not been encouraged by the coquetting which the secret envoy of Great Britain had had with the parties foremost in that insurrection. Lord Minto in Rome had encouraged the rioters there—those who had shown the first symptoms of setting the Pope's authority at nought. Lord Minto had entertained at his own table Sterbini and the men now connected with the hideous outrages of that unfortunate insurrection. It would be for Ministers to clear themselves, and prove that they were not responsible for those outrages, by the kind of authority and encouragement which the secret envoy of this country had given to those parties in Rome. And yet not one word was there in the Royal Speech to express the slightest sympathy for the Pope, who had been driven from his throne by a band of assassins, the vilest and meanest of mankind. [100]

John O'Connell was very close to his father Daniel O'Connell. He had been imprisoned by Sir Robert Peel in 1843 at the same time as his father. He would have known of his father's intentions in

---

[99] House of Commons Debate, *Destitute Persons (Ireland) Bill.* 08 February 1847.

[100] House of Commons Debate, *Address in answer to the Queen's speech.*(the Queen's speech). 05 February 1849.

going to see the Pope in Rome. He would have watched closely the political intrigues around Pope Pius the ninth. His accusations may have contained some element of truth.

THE MAN WOT PLAYS SEVERAL INSTRUMENTS
AT ONCE.

In this cartoon from Punch, in 1845, Sir Robert Peel is shown playing several instruments at once. "Sliding Scale" is written on the bells at the back, "free trade" is on his hat, "tariffs" is around his neck, "Income Tax" is on the cymbals between his legs, and Maynooth Grant is on the drum. The grant to the Catholic Seminary in Maynooth was an important part of the policy of Sir Robert Peel towards Ireland. Lord Russell looks on.

Image courtesy of the National Library of Ireland.

William Smith O' Brien and the failed Revolution

William Smith O'Brien was one of the few leaders in Ireland who tried to lead a revolt in 1848. In February 1848 there was a revolution in France, and the monarchy of King Louis Phillipe was overthrown. Smith O'Brien and Thomas Meagher (Meagher of the sword) and Richard O'Gorman went to Paris to meet with Lamartine, the poet President of the new French Republic. Lamartine had offered support to other oppressed nations of Europe in a document prepared by the new French Government, called a "Manifesto to Europe". The three Irish delegates met with Lamartine on 17 March 1848 and accepted the tricolour flag from him. When this was reported in the Times of 20 March 1848, the British Ambassador, Lord Normanby, immediately put pressure on the French not to give any support to the Irish.

Smith O Brien came back to the House of Commons in April 1848, shortly after his visit to France. It was a daring appearance after such an act of defiance of the government of Lord Russell. He gave a speech in the House of Commons on 10 April 1848 which deserves to be remembered alongside the speeches of Robert Emmet and Patrick Pearse. He said

I would gladly accept the most ignominious death that could be inflicted upon me, rather than witness the sufferings and the indignities that I have seen inflicted by this Legislature upon my countrymen during the last thirty years of my life. …I am here to tell you to-night that I sincerely believe, if you refuse those claims during the present year, you will have to encounter the chance of a republic in Ireland. I do not profess disloyalty to the Queen of England. But if it is treason to profess disloyalty to this House, and to the government of Ireland by the Parliament of Great Britain—if that be treason, I avow the treason. Nay, more, I say it shall be the study of my life to overthrow the dominion of this Parliament over Ireland. Now, I avow the fact—I know not whether it be illegal or not—that I have been instrumental in asking my countrymen to arm. I conceive that under the present circumstances of all nations, it is the duty of every man to obtain the possession, and to learn the use of arms. There is not a nation, I believe, in Europe, which does not make it part of its duty to instruct its citizens in the use of arms; and I conceive that it is the peculiar duty of the Irish people to obtain the possession of arms at a time when you tell them you are prepared to crush their expression of opinion, not by argument, but by brute force. We hereby declare that our object is now, as it always was, the legislative independence of Ireland, and thereby the attainment of social order; and we desire that such independence may be obtained, if possible, without civil war.

Before the knell of English power in Ireland is sounded, I beg of you to make friends of the Irish people, by conceding to them those national rights which they claim, and to which, by every right, human and divine, they are entitled.

When the noble Lord tells me I am a traitor to the Crown, I repel the charge, and retort it. I tell him, it is not I, but he and his Colleagues, that are traitors to the country, the Queen and the constitution.[101]

In July 1848, Smith O Brien set out to lead an insurrection. He decided that it should be inland and away from English warships. The threat of these warships had caused Daniel O Connell to cancel a Monster Meeting at Clontarf in October 1843. Smith O Brien went to Tipperary where he was

---

[101] House of Commons Debate, *Crown and Government Security Bill*. 10 April 1848.

promised support. One of the people he relied on to join him was Fr. John Kenyon (1812-1869) a priest from Templederry in Tipperary. This priest was a member of the group of Confederation Clubs. These Clubs had been established early in 1848 by William Smith O'Brien, to train men in how to use arms. Fr. Kenyon was very much in favour of revolt. When O Brien asked Fr. Kenyon to lead out his men, the priest refused. It appears that Fr. Kenyon was threatened by his Bishop that he would be excommunicated from the church if he joined with O Brien. For a Catholic, this would be an excommunication forever from the core beliefs of his life. It was a cruel threat to Fr. Kenyon. Years later, in 1866, he met John Mitchel in Paris, and said how much he regretted not coming. Kenyon, Mitchell, and William Smith O'Brien were all outmanoeuvred by Russell.

There was a skirmish at Ballingarry, County Tipperary on 29 July 1848, where two of O'Brien's men were killed by militia. O Brien called the revolt off. He was later arrested, and sentenced to be hanged, drawn and quartered. This was an embarrassment to the Russell government. It would not look well to have a Member of Parliament hanged drawn and quartered. The law was changed. O'Brien was sentenced instead to deportation to Van Dieman's Land.

There was considerable sympathy for William Smith O'Brien in Ireland. 80,974 people signed petitions for his release. These petitions are now important historic documents, which help people to trace their ancestors in Ireland.

He had been one of the main critics of the operation of the Poor Laws in Ireland. He had constantly pointed out how they were failing. He said

> it appeared that the object of the Government, and of the Poor Law Commissioners, was to render the large expenditure upon the poor of that country as unproductive as possible. He was afraid that after expending millions the result would, on looking back, be found to have been a mere waste of money, and that its expenditure had been productive of no other consequence than that of the demoralisation of the people.

He pointed out that the government must change its policies.

> His object in rising chiefly was to make an appeal to the Government, not to allow the people of Ireland to die as they were now dying.[102]

James Joyce commemorated Smith O Brien in "Ulysses"

> The funeral cortege for Dignam passes along O'Connell St., Leopold Bloom notices the statue of Smith O'Brien. Someone has laid a bunch of flowers there. Woman. Must be his death day. For many happy returns. The carriage wheeling by Farrell's statue united noiselessly their unresisting knees. (Wonder why he was struck off the rolls.) Had his office in Hume St. Same house as Molly's namesake. Tweedy. Terrible comedown poor wretch! Kicked about like snuff at a wake.[103]

William Smith O'Brien was given a limited pardon in 1854, on condition that he did not return to Ireland. He lived in Brussels for two years and returned to Ireland in 1856. He died in Wales on 16

---

[102] House of Commons Debate, *The State of Ireland.* 09 February 1848.

[103] James Joyce, *Ulysses.* 1922, Paris. Page 83.

June 1864 at the age of 60. (The day he died, on 16 June, is Bloomsday in Joyce's Ulysses.) He had made a significant protest against English rule, which inspired many generations after him.

His words were influential on Patrick Pearse, and the men of 1916, who led an armed rebellion against the English Parliament, and who declared a Republic. The flag, the tricolour, which William Smith O'Brien and Thomas Francis Meagher had received from Lamartine, was first flown in Ireland over the General Post Office (the GPO) in 1916. The protest of William Smith O'Brien affected future generations of Irishmen. In particular, his protests were against the injustice of the Poor Laws of Lord Russell. He is an eloquent witness to the harm which was caused by the building of 161 workhouses in Ireland, and by the implementation of the Poor Laws.

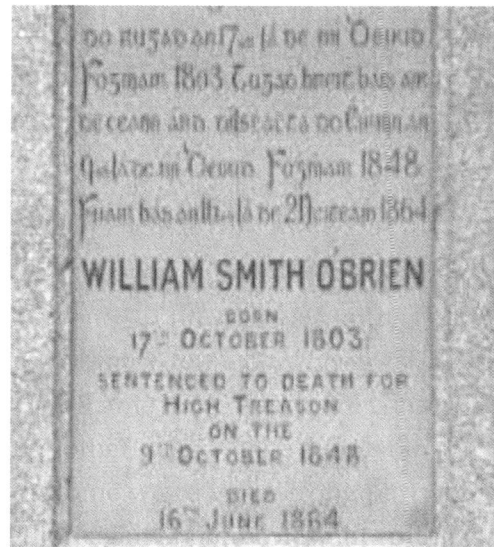

The statue, (by Farrell), of William Smith O Brien, in O'Connell Street in Dublin.

There is a description on the base of the statue of William Smith O'Brien which says that he was sentenced to death for high treason on 9 October 1848. The court sentenced him to be hanged drawn and quartered. The Parliament changed the law and he was sent into exile in Van Diemen's land.

Trevelyan Our Subordinate Officer

It has become customary to put the blame for the maladministration during the famine on Sir Charles Trevelyan (1807-1886), but it is time to reassess his role. He was the head of the Civil Service, but he was not the person who created the policies which led to the famine. No civil servant will last very long if he mistakes his position and dictates policy to his political masters. Trevelyan was the epitome of the safe pair of hands, a civil servant who could be relied on to interpret the wishes of his Prime Minister and his party, and to carry them out without question. Trevelyan was Under Secretary of the Treasury from 1840 until 1859. He served Lord Russell faithfully and carried out his policies well. He was not, however the architect of the policies. The policies were dictated by Sir Robert Peel and Lord John Russell. Russell himself declared in the House of Commons

> But I must say, that whilst Mr. Trevelyan has acted with intelligence, with judgement, and I am sure with indefatigable and untiring zeal, yet, in regard to the orders which he has received, if any blame is to be laid- if any censure is to be cast, let that blame and that censure fall upon us and not upon our subordinate officer.[104]

Trevelyan came from a religious family. His father was the Archdeacon of Taunton, in Somerset. He was educated at Hailebury, at the East India School, where he was taught by Thomas Malthus. He then served in the Indian Civil Service from 1826 to 1840.

In 1834, his political master was the writer Thomas Babington Macaulay. Macaulay was on the Supreme Council of India. It was the fervent wish of Macaulay that the people of India should adopt English as a common language. Up to that time there was a wide variety of languages spoken in India. Macaulay wrote a "Minute on Indian Education" in February 1835. In this minute he wrote " a single shelf of a good European library was worth the whole native literature of India and Arabia". In 1835 Macaulay passed legislation to make English the spoken language in India. The word "Macaulayism" is understood in India to mean colonising through imposing a foreign language on a people. In 1838, Trevelyan published a book reiterating the policies of Macaulay. His book was called "On the Education of the people of India".

Trevelyan married Hannah, the sister of Macaulay, in 1834. In 1839, Macaulay was appointed Secretary of War in the Government in London. In 1840 Trevelyan was brought home from India and was appointed Under Secretary of the Treasury. The timing may be a coincidence, but Macaulay had influence with the government and may have wished to have his sister and her family back in England. The post of Under Secretary of the Treasury was effectively the post of the head of the Civil Service. There were two actual Secretaries of the Treasury, but these were serving Members of Parliament.

While serving as Under Secretary, Trevelyan carried out the policies of Lord Russell conscientiously. In 1848 he published a book on "The Irish Crisis", which echoed the policies of Lord Russell. He started the book by emphasising that the majority of the Irish people were dependent on the potato. He continued by saying that the calamity of the famine would be seen by future generations as a blessing.

---

[104] House of Commons Debate, *Address in answer to the speech*. 19 January 1847.

Unless we are much deceived, posterity will trace to that Famine the commencement of a salutary revolution in the habits of a nation long singularly unfortunate, and will acknowledge that on this, as on many other occasions, Supreme Wisdom has educed permanent good out of transient evil.[105]

This was a sentiment which Lord Russell also expressed in Parliament. In 1848, Trevelyan received a knighthood for this book.

Henry Grattan criticised the book in Parliament. He said

He held in his hand a book, called "The Irish Crisis", which he was informed was published and circulated at the expense of the government. ... This book, however was written by an Englishman, high in favour with the Government. It commenced and ended with mis statement... here was an English gentleman who had been made a knight, and rewarded by a vote of 2,000L for writing a book which added insult to injury as far as the Irish nation was concerned. [106]

Trevelyan continued as Under Secretary of the Treasury until 1859. The Government of Lord Russell fell in 1852. Trevelyan then became occupied with a report on reforming the Civil Service. This he wrote together with Sir Stafford Northcote. It was published in November 1853. The report was called "The Organisation of the Permanent Civil Service". It laid the foundation for appointments to be made to the Civil Service by written competition, instead of through political favour. Trevelyan is credited with the initiatives in this report. But this initiative was taken under the guidance of William Gladstone, the Chancellor of the Exchequer. It was Gladstone who wrote the terms of reference for the report. It was Gladstone who set up a Civil Service Commission in 1855 as a result of the report. Again, Trevelyan was carrying out the wishes of his political masters.

In 1859 Trevelyan returned to India, where he was appointed Governor of Madras. Lord Russell became Foreign Secretary from June 1859 to November 1865. Trevelyan was again working in close contact with him. In 1859 also, the Government sent out James Wilson, the former Editor of the Economist, to organise the collection of taxes in India, and in particular to impose an income tax on the population of India, which then comprised 150,000,000 people. Trevelyan opposed the imposition of income tax in his province, Madras, and made his views publically known. It was regarded as an act of subordination, and he was relieved of his duties. It was Lord Russell who had him recalled.[107]

Within two years he was again in India as Finance Minister. It is difficult to know whether he had really been dismissed or whether there was some political manoeuvring going on. It would seem he was still carrying out the wishes of his political masters.

In 1853, the Irish M.P. George Moore, summed up the characteristics of Trevelyan. He said

this self-satisfied functionary seems utterly unable to conceive the possibility of his having ever made a mistake, even the most trifling. To be sure nothing that he undertook succeeded—nothing that he anticipated came to pass—disaster followed every scheme he originated - and he aggravated every disaster by the remedies he applied.

---

[105] Charles Trevelyan, *The Irish Crisis*. 1848 London.

[106] House of Commons Debate, *Relief of distress Ireland.* February 12 1849.

[107] House of Commons Debate, *Recall of Sir Charles Trevelyan.* 11 May 1860.

Trevelyan had given evidence to a House of Lords Inquiry in 1852.[108] The inquiry questioned the policies during the famine. Trevelyan justified the policies. Moore said

> if there was a man in the country more willing than another—if there was a man more able than another, to dissuade the Committee from adopting the recommendation contained in this Report, it was undoubtedly Sir C. Trevelyan; and anyone who has taken the trouble to read his evidence will see that he spared nothing, and scrupled nothing, to effect that object.

Moore denounced the attitude of Trevelyan in eloquent prose

> I do not deny the abilities and energies of Sir C. Trevelyan; still less do I doubt the rectitude of his motives and intentions; but energy in a mistake is only an aggravation, and the rectitude in which a great injury is inflicted is but a small consolation to the injured.[109]

Moore was the father of George Moore, the author. It is evident that George inherited his literary ability from his father.

The inquiry in 1852 was critical of the evidence of Charles Trevelyan, and disagreed with his arguments about the policies which had been carried out during the Famine.

---

[108] House of Commons Report. (585). Select Committee on Consolidated Annuities. Evidence of Trevelyan Page 157 of 812. (101 in original), Tuesday 20 April 1852. In University of Southampton, Enhanced British Parliamentary Papers on Ireland. www.dippam.ac.uk/eppi/documents/13234.

[109] House of Commons Debate, Consolidated Annuities (Ireland). 07 April 1853 vol 125 cc 745

The Rate in Aid

In 1849 Lord Russell introduced a new tax on Ireland. It was called the "Rate in Aid." It was to be "in aid" of the distressed Unions. Russell proposed that every Union in Ireland should raise an extra 6 pence on top of the rates which they would normally charge, and give this money to the distressed Unions.

There were 22 distressed Unions in the West of Ireland, who could not afford to maintain the paupers who came to them, and who found it impossible to collect the rates. In addition, there were about ten other Unions who were in strained circumstances, and who needed some help.

For many Landlords this Rate in Aid was the final straw. Already they were paying very high rates for their tenants who could not afford to pay rents. It was more than they could bear, to have to pay an extra 6 pence in the £1 on top of the rates already imposed. In addition, the Boards of Guardians were not consulted by Lord Russell about this rate, and they were not consulted about how it should be spent. Many M.P.s expressed their objections in Parliament, and said that it was unfair, and that it would put an extra burden on those who were just managing to collect the taxes.

The rate which was paid by every Union in Ireland was already very onerous. A report from the Under Secretary for Ireland in 1848 showed the amount of tax, £300,071, which was collected in 1846, and that this trebled in 1847 to £970,318.[110] A further report stated that the total amount of rates collected in Ireland between 1843 and May 1848 was £2,304,561. Very few Unions were in arrears. This was money which had never before been raised in taxes in Ireland. It is not a coincidence that this money was raised and there was also a famine in Ireland at the same time.

In the debates which were held in Parliament about the Rate in Aid, the Irish members condemned the Poor Laws. If there was ever any doubt in the minds of future generations that the people at the time of the famine blamed the Poor Laws for the famine, this debate should make it very clear that the Poor Laws were considered to be the main cause by the opinion makers of the day. Fitzstephen French said

> He thanked the right hon. Baronet (the Chancellor of the Exchequer) for his sympathy with the western parts of Ireland; but begged to tell him that it was the Government's present specific, the poor-law, which was destroying the farmer, demoralising the peasantry, annihilating the property of the landlords, and which would not leave a vestige of the capital expended by the Imperial Parliament in that country in improvements.[111]
> the fact being that the blame was due to that House-to English statesmen who had forced a law upon Ireland (the Poor Law) which it was not fitted for.[112]

Poulett Scrope also said that the Poor Law had failed

The Poor Law had been passed with the view of preventing such loss of life from taking

---

[110] Parliamentary Papers, Poor Law (Ireland) *Copy of a letter from the Poor Law Commissioners Ireland.* 7 February 1848.

[111] House of Commons Debate, *Relief of Distress (Ireland).* 07 February 1849 vol 102, cc 398.

[112] House of Commons Debate, *Poor-Relief (Ireland) Bill.* 8 June 1849 cc 1315.

place, but as at present administered it failed to do so.... Mr. Ward, of Ballinasloe, stated that more than 700 families were wandering about the neighbourhood without a house to cover them, seeking shelter in the ditches at night, and then dying there, and then buried without coffins, after being perhaps disfigured by rats and dogs. ... He begged to ask the noble Lord (Lord Russell) whether ...he did not think the responsibility attached to the Government to bring forward such measures as may be necessary.[113]

Lord Russell had a majority of the votes in the House of Commons. The Rate in Aid Bill was carried. Much of the money raised was spent in paying for the poor to emigrate from the distressed districts of Mayo, Kerry and Donegal.

---

[113] House of Commons Debate, *Famine in Ireland.* 25 May 1849 vol 105 cc.987.

At last, an inquiry into the operation of the Poor Laws in Ireland

The Irish M.P.s had frequently requested an inquiry into the operation of the Poor Laws in Ireland. In 1849 Lord Russell finally agreed, possibly because of the revolt of William Smith O'Brien, or possibly because he had already got what he wanted. There were two Commissions of Inquiry set up, one in the House of Commons and one in the House of Lords. In the House of Commons, Lord Russell was in control. He announced at this Inquiry that he reserved the right to introduce his own initiatives, even if the Commission of Inquiry did not agree with him. It was during this inquiry that he introduced his scheme for the Rate in Aid. He sabotaged that inquiry.

The Inquiry in the House of Lords was a different matter altogether. A few days after Lord Russell announced that there would be a House of Commons inquiry into the operation of the Poor Laws in Ireland, Lord Melbourne announced in the House of Lords that they also would hold an inquiry. This inquiry was a most thorough and incisive inquiry into the causes of the famine, and into how the people were treated in the years from 1840 to 1849. All the people who were prominent in the administration of Ireland during that time were called to give evidence. The people who were asking the questions were also closely connected with Ireland. Sometimes, the Earl St. Germans was leading the inquiry. He was Edward Granville Eliot, 3rd Earl of St. Germans, who had been Chief Secretary for Ireland from 1841 to 1845, and also became Lord Lieutenant of Ireland at a later date. Sometimes the Lord Steward was in the chair. He was the Earl Fortescue, who had been Lord Lieutenant of Ireland from 1839 to 1841, at the time when George Nicholls was in Ireland setting up the workhouses.

One of the first people called was George Nicholls, who had come to Ireland in 1838 to establish the workhouses. He said that he was very much against the giving of outdoor relief to the poor. In his opinion the workhouses were an effective way of dealing with those who were in distress. However, he said, workhouses were never intended to deal with a great calamity such as the famine. He said that he had left Ireland in 1842, and had very little knowledge of what had happened there since then.

Sir Richard Griffith was called, and he said that it was clear that there were different rates charged in different parts of the country. He said that the Boards of Guardians relied on the maps which were drawn up by the Ordnance Survey of the military in previous years to impose rates on the population. He said the rateable valuation was generally 20% less than the annual rental value of the land.

The Count Strzelecki was called. He said that he had served in Ireland for eighteen months, as an executive officer of the British Relief Association, and afterwards for two months as agent of the Treasury to administer the remainder of the relief. His time working for the British Association ended in June 1848, and he remained in Ireland for two months to distribute money for the Treasury.

His dealings were mainly with twenty five distressed Unions in the West. He was asked about the attendance of Guardians at the Westport workhouse, and he said that he never attended meetings of the Boards. After June 1847 he never travelled around the country. He said "I left the most distressed Unions in June 1847, and Ireland in September last." (That is in September 1848)[114]. For the

---

[114] 1849 (365), *Fourth Report from the Select Committee of the House of Lords appointed to inquire into the operation of the Irish Poor Law*. Page 333 of 384. Line 8543.

remainder of the time he stayed in Dublin. He said that the living conditions of the poor Irish in the West of Ireland were the worst of anything he had seen in his travels around the world.

> I have not found anywhere else men subject to misery of such an aggravated character as the Irish peasantry of the Western Unions were... Still the painful and frequent occurrence of corpses lying in the streets of some towns, and on the great roads, stamps that distress with a severity far exceeding that which accompanied and resulted from the great famine in Tuscany in 1346, 1347, 1349, as narrated by Sismondi.[115]

He was asked, if the bodies of the dead, lying in the streets, was an unusual sight? He replied

> It was very usual, as was also the absence of the habitual sensation which such sight commonly creates amongst the inhabitants, and for which the frequency of such melancholy occurrences may partly account.

He said that the worst time during the famine was the time between when the Public Works which took place under the Labour Rate Act were stopped, and the Temporary Relief Act under General Burgoyne came into effect.[116]

General Burgogyne was also called to give evidence. He described how he had been Chairman of the Office of Public Works in Ireland from 1831 to 1845, when he had retired. He told of his work in building bridges and harbours in Ireland during that time. He had supervised the building of Kingston Harbour (now Dun Laoire) and the Shannon Navigation Scheme. He was asked about his opinion of the Public Works which had taken place under the Labour Rate Act. He said

> They were perfectly useless and worse than useless very often, from the mode in which they were necessarily carried on... In very many ways those works were attended with very injurious effects. First, when the necessity for them as a medium of relief having ceased, they were abruptly relinquished, the object for which they were commenced as works being only partly accomplished: for instance, a road-way half cut through, or excavations for drainage, only carried out for a portion of the entire project.[117]

He said that the system of distributing free food under the Temporary Relief Act was at least straightforward. People were given one pound of meal per adult and a half pound per child.

He was asked if the Public Works had the effect of taking labourers away from their normal work of tilling the ground to grow vegetables, and he replied

> They do, to a certain extent. It was one of the accusations made at the time of the Labour Rate Act, that giving people employment on the roads meant that the land would not be prepared for growing crops, and that it would lead to famine the following year".

---

[115] Parliamentary Papers (365), *Fourth Report from the Select Committee of the House of Lords appointed to inquire into the operation of the Irish Poor Law*. Page image 336 of 384 May 1849 (line 8571).

[116] Parliamentary Papers (365), *Fourth Report from the Select Committee of the House of Lords appointed to inquire into the operation of the Irish Poor Law*. Page image 336 of 384 May 1849 (line 8574).

[117] Parliamentary Papers 1849 (365), *Fourth report from the Select Committee of the House of Lords appointed to inquire into the operation of the Irish Poor Law*. 4 May 1849. Page image 350 of 384. (line 8694).

Burgogyne's evidence, and the questions asked of him, would seem to reinforce this argument.

He was asked if Sir Charles Trevelyan had come to visit him in Ireland in October 1847. He said yes, Trevelyan had come for a few days. He was asked if he had prepared a statement for publication in the press, to be given to Trevelyan. He said yes. A copy of this statement was included in the book of evidence. By its style it would seem as if it was written by Trevelyan himself. It stated that although the potato blight did not affect the crop in 1847, only one sixth of the amount of potatoes which were normally planted had been sown, and therefore there would continue to be hardship in Ireland.

> Although the potatoes have succeeded better this year than on the two former, not above one-sixth of the usual quantity has been planted, and that not by the small occupiers, as usual, for their support, because the case appeared hopeless, and even otherwise the seed was wanting.[118]

The letter ended on a strange note, which does not read as if it were written by Colonel Burgoyne. It said that Ireland needed social change if it was to prosper in the future, and people must expect this.

> But along the West, very active and extended benevolence is required to be exerted from elsewhere, to prevent the most horrible scenes: that this calamity is continuous, and can only be gradually removed by a new order in the social system, which it will be the interest, and must be the effort, of all parties to introduce and to accelerate.

This sentiment is exactly that which Lord Russell and Sir Robert Peel put forward in the House of Commons debate on the Incumbered Estates Act. It may have seemed necessary to them to send Trevelyan to Ireland to justify their policies.

The most important witness was Edward Boyd Twisleton, the Poor Law Commissioner for Ireland. He told the House of Commons Inquiry in March 1849 that he had resigned two weeks earlier, in protest at the measure introduced by Lord Russell to impose a Rate in Aid. He described the organisation of the workhouses, and he said that they should never have been looked on as a solution to a famine. In the case of a famine, the Imperial Government should have stepped in to help the population. It should not have been a matter of raising a local rate on the people who were suffering from starvation. He said that the Rate in Aid would cause resentment amongst the Unions who were doing their best to pay for their own workhouses, and who asked why were the distressed Unions not paying their own way, were their landlords not paying their share of the rates?

It was in the inquiry in the House of Lords that Twisleton made the statement that no one need have died. He was asked

> Independently of Poor Law principles, are there other appliances which your experience in Ireland… would lead you to suggest as being remedies …for the prevention and check of pauperism?
> He replied

---

[118] Parliamentary Papers, 1849(365), *Fourth report from the Select Committee of the House of Lords appointed to inquire into the operation of the Irish Poor Law.* 4 May 1849, page 354 of 384. Paragraph 8726.

I am anxious to make no suggestion involving the expenditure of public money, which might divert attention from the comparatively trifling sum with which it is possible for this country to spare itself the deep disgrace of permitting any of our miserable fellow subjects in the Distressed Unions to die of starvation. I want to leave it distinctly on record that no one need have died of famine in Ireland. For a fraction of the cost of the Kaffir War, we can be spared the shame of letting our fellow citizens die. *[119]*

If Edmund Twisleton, who was at the centre of the organisation of the Poor Laws in Ireland from 1845 to 1849 has made a statement of this nature, it must be believed. He made this statement for future generations of Irish people. He resigned in protest at the policies of Lord Russell and Sir Robert Peel. There can be no more eloquent voice than his. We can only acknowledge his generosity of spirit in putting it on record for future generations of Irish people that this was the truth about the famine. No one need have died.

_____

[119] Parliamentary Papers 1849 (365), *Fourth report from the Select Committee of the House of Lords appointed to inquire into the operation of the Irish Poor Law.* 24 April 1849. Page 200 of 384 (717 in the original). Paragraph 7444.

THE ENGLISH LABOURER'S BURDEN;

OR, THE IRISH OLD MAN OF THE MOUNTAIN.

[See *Sinbad the Sailor.*

The cartoons in Punch often showed the Irishman with the features of a monkey. In this cartoon in 1849, the Irishman is seen riding on the back of the poor English Labourer. Twisleton condemned these cartoons.

Image courtesy of the National Library of Ireland.

Edward Boyd Twisleton: the only official man with a conscience.

Edward Turner Boyd Twisleton (1809-1876) was born in Ceylon. His father was the archdeacon of Columbo. He was a distinguished scholar and a lawyer. In November 1845 he was appointed Commissioner for the administration of the Irish Poor Laws. He was of the family of Lord Saye and Sele. His grandfather was Thomas Twisleton, Baron Saye and Sele. In 1847, his elder brother succeeded to the title. Twisleton was a conscientious Civil Servant. He was also a man of compassion. The author Thomas Carlyle referred to Edward Twisleton as "the only official man in whom I find clear continual evidence of a conscience."[120]

Twisleton had already shown great moral courage in the course of his administration of the Poor Laws for Ireland, in countermanding the Gregory clause in the Poor Law Extension Act. This clause had come into operation on 1 November 1847. Many thousands had been evicted. Twisleton challenged the clause. He asked for legal advice from the Attorney General for Ireland, James Monahan, and from the Queen's Counsel in Ireland, Jonathan Henn. He asked if the wife and family of a farmer who refused to give up his land could gain admission to a workhouse, even if the farmer would not give up his land.

He collected information about families who had starved to death rather than give up their small holdings. One of the cases was of a Co. Leitrim woman, Wabby McSweeney, from Aughacashel near Ballinamore. In April 1848 she was found dead in a ditch on her way back home to her family. She had collected a quarter stone of oatmeal from "the paupers" (the relieving officer of the workhouse) to feed her children. The evidence given at the autopsy was that her husband refused to give up his small farm, even though the family were starving.[121]

Jonathan Henn gave an opinion that the wife and children were not owners or tenants of such farms, and that they would be entitled to claim relief. There was a debate about Twisleton's interpretation of the law in the House of Lords. The members were indignant. The Duke of Richmond protested that a man who did not support his family should be punished. (The Duke was a brother of Lord Russell). He said

> If the Irish Attorney and Solicitor General were right in their view of the law, then he would advise the Government to bring in a Bill enacting, that should the wives or children of any holder of land accept relief, the title to the land should thereby be forfeited. If he were an Irish magistrate, he should punish the holders of such land with the utmost severity.[122]

Lord Mounteagle also was outraged. He quoted the opinion of Jonathan Henn in the House of Lords

> The opinion went on to state, that if the father, notwithstanding his possession of the land, is really unable to maintain the children, I do not think he could be properly convicted under the 10th and 11th of Victoria, cap. 84, section 2.

---

[120]Thomas Carlyle Letters. Volume 28 letter 238. www.carlyleletters .dukeupress.edu, We can only agree with the judgement of Carlyle.

[121] Parliamentary Papers, 1847-1848 (442), Poor Law (Ireland). *Copies of the Correspondence upon which the Commissioners for the Poor Laws in Ireland took legal advice.* Page image 1 of 6.

[122] House of Lords Debate, *Irish Poor law.* 19 June 1848.

Lord Mounteagle objected to this opinion

If that opinion were correct, the possession of land was no test as to the propriety of giving relief at all. Yet Parliament intended it to be a final and conclusive test. The intention of the Legislature was, that the possession of land should exclude the plea of destitution. The opinion of Mr. Henn, backed by that of Mr. Monahan, was, that the possession of land did not exclude the plea of destitution. Those Gentlemen, however, recommended that every case should be decided on its own merits before boards of guardians. Why, this was opening the door as wide as if they had never passed an Act to shut it at all.

The Marquess of Lansdowne said:-

He quite agreed with his noble Friend that of all abuses connected with the administration of the poor-laws none could be greater than that the wives and children of men who held land should go to a public charity for relief; he therefore thought that no time should be lost in issuing an order that assistance should not in future be given to such persons, or those naturally dependent on them.

The Marquess of Lansdowne held lands in Kerry. He certainly did not want to have to pay a larger amount of rates for his tenants who might be starving, and who might go to a workhouse, and yet did not wish to give up their land.

The decision of Edward Twisleton to challenge the legislation of his Prime Minister Lord Russell, and to allow the families of destitute farmers to go to a workhouse, undoubtedly saved a lot of lives. It showed moral courage, and an independence of mind in one who could have meekly continued to administer the law. Instead of continuing to carry out the policies of Lord Russell in Ireland, he resigned.

The report of the Poor Law Commissioners for 1849 records a tribute from the Irish staff of the Poor Law Commissioners to Edward Twisleton. They described

Our deep sense of the loss which the Commission has sustained in the retirement of the late Chief Commissioner Mr. Twisleton whose high talents and entire devotion to the duties of his office could not be so truly estimated by any parties as by those who acted with him.

It was signed by Alfred Power, Wm Somerville and T.N. Redington, Poor Law Commissioners for Ireland. He was indeed, an official man with a conscience.

THE NEW ST. PATRICK;

Or, SIR ROBERT TURNING THE REPTILES OUT OF IRELAND.

It was Sir Robert Peel who first suggested a plantation of Connaught, in a speech in the House of Commons in March 1849. Sir Robert Peel is depicted here in this cartoon in Punch as banishing all the bad things out of Ireland, such as Destitution, written on the snake which is slithering into the sea. Usury and Mortgages are written on the little man in the foreground. Peel holds in his hand a paper with the title "New Plantation".

Image courtesy of the National Library of Ireland.

The Plantation of Connaught

In 1849, while the inquiries were going on into the Poor Laws in Ireland, Lord Russell introduced another new project. This was the Incumbered Estates Act. He proposed that any Irish Landlord who was in debt of any kind, could be forced to sell his estate in order to pay this debt. His new Bill relaxed the laws relating to debt and made it easier to evict owners of land. It was an older version of today's schemes which enable vulture funds to sell the property of those in arrears with their mortgages.

During the course of this debate, Sir Robert Peel suggested that the land in the West of Ireland should be given over to new proprietors. He called this the "Plantation of Connaught". There had been a plantation of Ulster in the time of King James the First of England, in 1609. Peel praised the results of that plantation, which had created a population in the North of Ireland who were loyal to the crown.[123] He said

> Sir Arthur Chichester was the Lord Deputy at the period in question. He caused surveys to be made, and it was decided that the lands to be planted, as the term was, should be divided into allotments of 2,000, 1,500, and 1,000 English acres, respectively. These escheated lands were disposed of to 104 English and Scotch, 56 servitors, and 286 natives, all of whom gave bond to the Government for the performance of certain covenants. The Lord Deputy caused a parochial church to be erected, and a glebe set out, according to the size of the parish, for each incumbent. The plantation was extended to Leinster. In the course of these proceedings, through the misconduct of the agents employed, great injustice occasionally was done to individuals; but, says Carte—
>
> The grievances of particular persons did not prevent the general good intended to the kingdom by these plantations, in consequence of which lands were cultivated and greatly improved, towns and villages built, trade and commerce carried on and extended. The people in general, weaned gradually from their former idle and disorderly life, began to learn and practise civility, to apply themselves to business, to use labour and industry in their several stations, and to relish the sweets of peace.
>
> If it be possible to make any new settlement similar to that of Ulster, my earnest advice—an

---

[123] Footnote to the "Incumbered Estates Act":-When Sir Robert Peel proposed the Plantation of Connaught, he referred to the precedent of The Plantation of Ulster. This previous plantation took place during the reign of King James the First of England and the Sixth of Scotland in 1609. Lord Russell was a direct descendent of King James the First through the liaison of King Charles the Second and Louise de Kerouille.

When Peel proposed a Plantation of Connaught, giving James the First as a precedent, he was appealing to Lord Russell's sense of history and his pride in leaving a lasting legacy to his country, such as a social reorganisation of the sister country, Ireland.

I suggest that King James the First was the Hamlet of Shakespeare's play. James was the son of Mary Queen of Scots (1542-1587). Mary's second husband, Lord Darnley, was murdered and it was suspected that the murderer was Lord Bothwell. Mary quickly married Bothwell, after the murder of her husband. James was the son of Lord Darnley, who was murdered.

There is also a link between James and Denmark. James married Anne of Denmark and spent his honeymoon in Elsinore. James thus became the "Prince of Denmark". It is likely that Shakespeare was flattering the new King. Hamlet was most likely written in 1602. James 1 came to the throne of England in 1603.

advice in unison with the universal feelings of the House—would be, that no religious distinctions should be allowed to enter into the arrangement. It may, perhaps, be impossible to apply the principle of the arrangement to the extent to which it was carried in James I.'s time; but unless it be applied to some degree, there is little hope of the future improvement of Ireland.[124]

He suggested that new capitalists should take over the estates in Connaught. He said:

There is no country in the world which has better prospects than Connaught. I cannot doubt that such a Commission as I suggest would facilitate the amicable transfer of land—would bring parties together, and convince the present owners and creditors that there was no advantage to them in maintaining the present state of things. I believe that those who have land to dispose of would find not only individuals, but companies, in this metropolis, disposed to follow the example of the great companies of London in the time of James I.— disposed to do so not merely from the hope of gain, but from the desire to co-operate in the improvement of Ireland. But one thing is essential—a clear indisputable title to the property, above all, by facilitating the transfer of property from insolvent to solvent proprietors.

Disraeli referred to this proposal of the ""Plantation of Connaught" in the House of Commons and said that it would not work.

You cannot plant Englishmen in Connaught without protecting them. How are they to be protected—by force—by their arming themselves? Let such a course be pursued, and instantly that will occur which has occurred in all plantations within the memory of man— there will be a development of the military principle. I cannot believe, Sir, that any attempt at home colonisation—any attempt to reproduce, even under a mitigated form, and under the modifying circumstances of the nineteenth century—any attempt to reproduce in the west of Ireland, a colony such as the Ulster plantation was in the north, can be attended but with heavy calamities, and perhaps the direst catastrophes.[125].

In his speech, Disraeli referred to Lord Russell in a derogatory tone

I hope the noble Lord at the head of the Government will be so kind as to wake from his slumber while I read that portion of the letter.

It is likely that Sir Robert Peel and Lord Russell were both in agreement about the proposals which were put forward in this scheme for the "Plantation of Connaught." There are cartoons in Punch in 1849 which suggest that this idea was proposed to Russell by Peel and that he was grateful to accept it. One cartoon showed Peel giving a gift to Russell with "Incumbered Estates" written on it. The other cartoon showed Peel as the new Saint Patrick, with his scheme for the Plantation of Connaught under his arm. Peel introduced his idea for the plantation of Connaught in the House of Commons on 30 March 1849. Three days later, on 2 April 1849, Lord Russell referred to it in a speech in the House of Commons on the Rate in Aid debate. Russell made a play of disagreeing with Sir Robert Peel. He said

100

---

[124] House of Commons Debate, *Poor-Laws (Ireland)-Rate in Aid-Adjourned Debate.* 05 March 1849 cc.171.

[125] House of Commons Debate, *Poor-Laws (Ireland)-Rate in Aid-Adjourned Debate (Third Night).* 02 April 1849.

Sir, I proceed to consider whether there would be any advantage in having a commission specially for the purpose of disposing of questions relating to land in the west of Ireland. It appears to me that such a commission must be one of two kinds: it must either have compulsory powers, or it must be merely of a voluntary nature. Of compulsory powers the right hon. Gentleman gave us an instance in the plan adopted with respect to the plantation of Ulster in the reign of James I. But there is this obvious difference—and the objection is so obvious that I think the right hon. Gentleman must have some answer to it—between that case and the present—in that case the land was at your disposal, and the people were not upon it; whereas, in the present case, the land is not at your disposal, and the people are upon it. Well then, Sir, it appears to me that it would be impossible for you to use the powers which were given in the times of James I to the commissioners whom he appointed—the lands having been then forfeited to the Crown, and the Crown having a full right to dispose of them.

Russell went on to say that a better plan would be to agree to the Incumbered Estates Act, so that land could be transferred to new owners with as little regulation as possible. He said

But the right hon. Gentleman touched upon another subject nearly connected with that to which I have just referred—and with respect to which I think Parliament may be able to effect very considerable improvements—I refer to those laws which encumber, and in many cases prevent, the transmission of property.[126]

Although he dismissed the idea of a "Plantation of Connaught", the essence of the idea was contained in the Incumbered Estates Act. This Act made it easier for landlords to be removed from their estates. A list of those landlords whose estates were sold is contained in the Parliamentary papers for 1850.[127]

This Act was passed at about the same time as the Rate in Aid became law. The money which was raised through that extra rate was mostly spent paying for people in the West of Ireland to emigrate. This idea was also contained in Peel's suggestion of a Plantation of Connaught. He said that it should be made easier to assist poor Irish labourers to emigrate. The fact that the extra money raised in the rate in aid was used to send people out of the country from the West of Ireland gives additional weight to the idea that Lord Russell and Sir Robert Peel planned to relocate English proprietors there.

When the Incumbered Estates Act was passed, notices began to appear in Irish newspapers of legal actions taken by debtors of Irish estates. Hundreds of claims were brought to the Commissioners. The value of estates dropped from twenty times the annual rental value, to ten times the annual value. Land to the value of £5,000,000 was forced onto the open market. So many claims were made that the whole legal process ground to a halt. In June 1852 the government came back to Parliament with a new Bill to extend the period of time which they had to dispose of these estates. The previous Bill had given them three years, and now they asked for another five years. Isaac Butt criticised the Incumbered Estates Act. He said

---

[126] House of Commons Debate, *Poor-Laws (Ireland)-Rate in Aid-Adjourned Debate (Third Night)*. 02 April 1849.

[127] Parliamentary Papers, Return of all sales made under the Authority of the Commissioners of Incumbered Estates, Ireland. See copy of one sample page in the appendix.

The Bill did not merely give facilities for selling—it extended the right of selling; and I ask the attention of the House to this fact, that it gave the right of selling property to persons who had never before possessed such right. If any man had a mortgage on an estate, no subsequent creditor could come in and sell the estate without being prepared to pay off the mortgage; but this Bill enabled any subsequent creditor to force the estate into the market without any reference to the mortgage.

Sir, I believe in my conscience that the operation of this Court has produced more individual misery and more individual wrong than any revolution that has ever taken place in any civilised country,… Out of 1,631 cases there are not 500 in which the Commissioners have finally adjudicated the rights of the different claimants to the money. The present sales amount to 5,000,000l., and out of that sum 2,500,000l. lies impounded in the Incumbered Estates Court, because the Commissioners have not been as yet able to decide the rights of the several parties claiming. They have 10,000,000l., in fact, to decide upon, and questions may arise in the distribution of this money as difficult as have ever yet arisen in any Court of Equity.

Isaac Butt had been elected a Member of Parliament in May 1852, and this was his maiden speech. He summed up the reasons why this Incumbered Estates Act should never have been passed

The measure was put into operation at a time when the country was suffering under the destroying influence of a prolonged famine. The change in the Corn Laws—whether wisely made or not I do not discuss—unquestionably lowered the value of land. The novel enactment of outdoor relief had imposed upon the land a burden the extent of which no one could see. This was not all. The circulating money of Ireland was diminished. The issue of bank-notes had diminished from 7,000,000l. in 1846, to 4,000,000l. in 1849. And just at that moment of unexampled depression, when everything conspired to depress the value of the soil, you passed a law to fling upon the market an amount of property for which even in the best times purchasers could not be found: you called an auction of the estate of every man who was in debt. The result has been what was to be expected. [128]

The pleas of the Irish M.P.s fell on deaf ears. The Incumbered Estates Act was renewed for a further five years. It was another part of the social reorganisation of Ireland and of the confiscation of land which took place under the administration of Lord Russell. Karl Marx referred to this Incumbered Estates Act as the third most important cause of the famine in Ireland. The other reasons he gave were firstly, the Repeal of the Corn Laws, and secondly, the introduction of the new Poor Law Act of 1847. [129]

For Lord Russell and also for Sir Robert Peel there was another priority included in the idea of the Plantation of Connaught. It was one of security against invasion from France. The threat which the French Revolution represented was all too keenly remembered by English politicians. They were aware that the French had sent help to Ireland in previous generaations. A loyal population on the West coast of Ireland would reduce that threat. Peel said

We have had the happiness to be exempted from the miseries which other countries of

---

[128] House of Commons Debate, *Incumbered Estates (Ireland) Bill.* 18 June 1852.

[129] Marx, Karl and Frederick Engels, *Ireland and the Irish Question.* (1869) Included in translation in R. Dixon (ed.) 1971 Moscow.

Europe had undergone from actual invasion. But recollect that during the last century, on three different occasions, since the year 1759, the attempts of France have been directed towards that very part of the united kingdom to the social improvement of which I am attaching so much importance. In 1759 an invasion of the west coast of Ireland, by a very formidable armament, was only defeated by the destruction of the French fleet under the command of M. de Conflans by Sir Edward Hawke. In 1796 a great effort was made by France to invade that part of Ireland in which one of the most distressed unions is situated. The descent on Bantry Bay was defeated by storms which dispersed the fleet of France. Again, in 1798, on the shores of another of those unions a landing was effected. The first town seized by the French after landing in the Bay of Killala was the town of Ballina. The small force which then landed, consisting of not more than 1,100 men, maintained their position in Ireland for seventeen days; and the town was in the possession of the French and rebel force for thirty-two days before they were finally expelled. I mention these facts for the purpose of reminding you that peace may not always be preserved; that you may have formidable combinations directed against you. We cannot conceal from ourselves— experience shows us—that this west coast of Ireland is the weak part of our empire. If we can by any decisive measures promote the happiness, contentment, and welfare of its inhabitants, we shall not only be promoting the internal peace and advancing the prosperity of Ireland, but, as Lord Bacon said, we shall be taking security that the weakness of that kingdom shall not, as heretofore, invite a foreign enemy to invasion.[130]

Peel concluded that the Plantation of Connaught would be a source of future security

"let us deeply consider whether "out of this nettle, danger, we may not pluck the flower, safety—and convert a grievous affliction into a means of future improvement and a source of future security".

Peel and Russell had worked very closely together during the time when Russell was Prime Minister. In fact the cartoons in Punch would suggest that Russell was really only acting as a puppet for Peel, in many of the policies which were put into effect during the famine. However, on 2 July, 1850, Sir Robert Peel died.

He regularly went riding along Constitution hill bedside Buckingham Palace. One evening, as he was riding past the entrance to Green Park, near Buckingham Palace, he raised his hat to a lady, and was thrown off his horse and killed. He was 60 years of age. From then on, the government of Lord Russell was never as resolute again. The tide began to turn for the Irish people.

---

[130] House of Commons Debate, *Poor-Laws (Ireland)-Rate in Aid-Adjourned Debate.* 30 March 1849.

PEEL'S PANACEA FOR IRELAND.

Russell. " Oh! this dreadful Irish Toothache! "
Peel. " Well, here is Something that will Cure you in an instant. "

This cartoon from Punch shows Sir Robert Peel suggesting the plan for the "Incumbered Estates Act" to Lord Russell. Russell: "Oh! this dreadful Irish Toothache!" Peel: "Well, here is Something that will Cure you in an instant." Peel is making a suggestion to Lord Russell that he should introduce an "Incumbered estates act" and that this will solve his problem by removing the Irish Landlords and repopulating Ireland with new English proprietors. It is Peel's panacea for Ireland.

Image courtesy of the National Library of Ireland.

GOG AND MAGOG GIVING PADDY A LIFT OUT OF THE MIRE.

"A Special Court of Common Council was held on Thursday to consider the propriety of purchasing estates in Ireland, with a view to cultivate and improve the same. * * * That London can and will do this work, her own history affords the most abundant guarantees."

Vide "Times," July 7.

This cartoon from Punch refers to Peels suggestion that English proprietors should be encouraged to come to Ireland, particularly Connaught, and to buy estates there. This would be facilitated by confiscating land from the Irish landlords through the "Incumbered Estates Bill". The cartoon is called "Gog and Magog giving Paddy a lift out of the mire. A special Court of Common Council was held on Thursday to consider the propriety of purchasing estates in Ireland, with a view to cultivate and improve the same. That London can and will do this work, her own history affords the most abundant guarantee." Vide Times July 7." Gog and Magog were figures in the bible that represented the enemies of the people. In Saxon folklore they were two giants. Punch cartoon 1849.

Image courtesy of the National Library of Ireland.

Tit for Tat. Lord Palmerston brought down Lord Russell.

In 1852 Lord Palmerston brought down the government of Lord Russell. It was a battle between two great Lords. On 24 December 1851, Lord Russell dismissed Lord Palmerston from the position of Foreign Secretary. Russell gave a speech on 3 February 1852 explaining why he had asked for the resignation of Palmerston. It all turned on the events in France. In December 1851, Louis Napoleon took over the National Assembly of those who had tried to bring democracy to France. He staged a coup and announced himself the ruler of the French.

Louis Napoleon was the nephew of Napoleon Bonaparte. Josephine had suggested to Napoleon that since they could not have children, her daughter and his brother could have a child who could be an heir for Napoleon. The marriage of Hortense Beauharnais and Joseph Napoleon was unhappy, but it did produce an heir. This was Louis Napoleon.

Palmerston evidently said in a private conversation with the French Ambassador in London that the coup of Louis Napoleon was probably the best outcome for France. Lord Russell said that Palmerston was indiscreet to say this, and therefore he forced him to resign.

Palmerston made a reply to this speech. He said that it was reported that Russell had also made similar remarks to the French Ambassador. He asked was he "to remain speechless like a gaping dolt or as silent as the mute of some Eastern Pasha" when the French Ambassador came to see him?" Russell prevailed, and Palmerston was dismissed as Foreign Secretary. From then on Palmerston worked behind the scenes to bring down Russell. On 20 February 1852, Russell introduced a Bill to recruit Local Militia throughout England. He proposed to conscript one in seven of all young men between the ages of 20 and 23, and to train them for a year, so that there would be a reserve military force in case of an invasion by France. Palmerston led an opposition to this bill, and it was defeated by 136 votes to 125. The government of Russell fell. The M.P. Henry Drummond said of the dispute between Russell and Palmerston that "it was not possible to interfere in a marriage or a fight." It appears there was an element of both in the relationship between Russell and Palmerston.

A new government was formed on 23 February 1852 under the leadership of Lord Derby. Then in July 1852 there was a general election. Things had changed in Ireland. A new group of Irish M.P.s were elected who agreed not to side with any party but to hold a balance of power to obtain better conditions for Ireland. They were mostly Catholic M.P.s. For the first time in the history of the British Parliament, a large group of Irish Catholic M.P.s formed a block to represent Irish interests. One of their objects was to obtain a cancelation of the huge debt which had been imposed by Lord Russell on Ireland, because of the Poor Laws, the building of the workhouses, and the famine. This group became known as "The Irish Brigade", or "The Pope's Brass Band." They called themselves the Independent Irish Party. They agreed before the election not to take office, but to exercise their power by voting together as a block. They had a different approach to that of the Irish M.P.s during the famine.

One of the reasons for the change was that the number of people with a vote had increased in Ireland. This was because of the repeated insistence by William Smith O'Brien that the way in which voters were registered should be changed. In the election of 1841, the number of people who were registered to vote in Ireland was 67,136. The number who were registered in 1852 was 181,188. The increase meant that more Irish Catholic M.P.s were elected to Parliament to represent Ireland.

There was an inequality in the way the seats in the House of Commons were allocated. In 1841 the population of England was 14,995,138 and they had 471 seats. The population of Ireland was 8,175,238 and they had 105 seats. Ireland with more than half the population of England had a quarter the number of seats. The population of Scotland at that time was 2,620,184, and of Wales was 911,603. Scotland had 53 seats and Wales had 29 seats. There were 658 seats in Parliament altogether. It was always going to be difficult for the Irish M.P.s to get legislation passed.[131]

The interim government, headed by the Earl of Derby, resumed power after the election of July 1852. In December 1852 the Irish Brigade brought this government down by voting against the budget. A new government headed by Lord Aberdeen came into power in December, and its government was announced in February 1853. The new government of Lord Aberdeen was prepared to deal with Ireland in a different and better way. They were also aware that the voting block of Irish M.P.'s in the Pope's Brass Band could bring them down.

---

[131] *Thoms Directory*, Dublin 1845, and 1852.

A Row among the "Pope's Brass Band". John Tenniel, Punch.

 The Pope's Brass Band was the name given to a group of Irish M.P.s. They were elected in 1852 to the Parliament in London. They forced the government in London to "drop the debt" in 1853. The Government cancelled all payment due for the building of the workhouses because of their actions. However, the group fell out amongst themselves. Two of their leaders, Sadlier and Keogh, accepted positions in the government of Lord Aberdeen, although they had pledged not to do so. This is portrayed in the cartoon. The faces of the two men who are well drawn in the cartoon resemble Sadlier and Keogh.

The new government forgave the debt.

Soon after the fall of Lord Russell's government, on 25 March 1852, Lord Monteagle asked the House of Lords to set up an inquiry into the repayment of debts from Ireland.[132] It was immediately agreed. It was a committee that had seven English Lords and six Irish Lords sitting on it. These included the Earl St. Germans who had been Lord Lieutenant of Ireland, and Lord Devon, who had chaired an Inquiry into the ownership of Irish land in 1845.

Lord Russell had given an estimate of the amount of money which he said Ireland owed to England as a result of the famine. The total amount was £4,483,000. He said

> The sums which are now due from Ireland to the Consolidated Fund are these:—Loans for building workhouses, 1,130,000l.; additional loans now being made for the same purpose, about 100,000l,; amount remaining unpaid for relief works under the 9th Victoria, cap. 1, about 158,000l.; amount unpaid under the 9th of Victoria, cap. 107, about 2,305,000l.; advances under the Temporary Relief Act, 790,000l.; making altogether 4,483,000l. By one of the Acts under which these loans were made, the Treasury were enabled to extend the repayments over a period of 20 years.[133]

Russell proposed that all these debts would be consolidated into one debt. This debt was to be repaid in annual repayments over a twenty year period. He called the debts "The Consolidated Annuities."

This was the situation which Lord Mounteagle asked the House of Lords Inquiry to examine. They published their conclusions in May 1852. These conclusions included one stating that the money which Lord Russell's government had spent on the Labour Rate Act had been worse than useless, and that the request to Ireland to repay that debt should be remitted. In other words, they recommended to "Drop the Debt."

The Independent Irish Party also added to the pressure on the government of Lord Aberdeen. There was every chance that they could bring down the government.

There were three leaders of the Independent Irish Party. These were William Keogh, M.P. for Athlone, John Sadlier, M.P. for Carlow, and George Henry Moore, M.P. for Roscommon. They had been elected to Parliament in 1852 on a pledge that they would not be aligned with any party, but would vote together as a block in the interests of Ireland. Unfortunately, both Sadlier and Keogh agreed to accept posts in the government of Lord Aberdeen. Sadlier accepted a post as Junior Lord of the Treasury, and Keogh accepted a post as Solicitor General for Ireland. Their names are still remembered in Irish history, as being synonymous with treachery.

It was left to George Moore to be the principal spokesman for the Irish Independent Party. This he did exceedingly well. He pressed hard for a cancellation of the debt supposedly due from Ireland for the Famine Relief works. He spoke about the "Labour Rate Act". He said "They could not have intended that, all seeking relief, no matter of what age or sex, or suffering from what bodily infirmity,

---

[132] . House of Commons. H.C. (585). *Select Committee on Consolidated Annuities.* Report from the Select Committee of the House of Lords. Brought from the Lords 1 July 1852.

[133]House of Commons Debate, *Distressed-Unions-advances-and-repayment.* 15 February 1850.

old and decrepid men, shivering women and children, should be all turned out in the snows and rains of winter to die of cold and exposure, in order that they might be saved from famine".

Moore put the blame on the Government of that time, the Government of Lord Russell

> the Executive and the Legislature acted, in the first instance, not without warning, continued to act afterwards in the teeth of conviction, and became therefore responsible for the consequences that ensued.

He condemned the fact that Ireland had to repay the money spent on the Labour Rate Act.

> But to profess to lend men money to be repaid with interest, and at the same time to insist that it shall be spent in the manner least profitable to the borrower, is a mode of dealing between man and man which it requires all the omnipotence of Parliament to justify.[134]

On 18 April 1853, Gladstone, the new Chancellor of the Exchequer, announced in his budget speech, that his government was remitting all the debt that Ireland owed to England, which was incurred because of the Poor Laws, and because of the relief works during the famine. He said

> The plan of the Government is that from and after 29th of last September the Consolidated Annuities shall be wholly wiped away. The whole sum due from Ireland to England shall be remitted. [135]

He proposed to introduce a system of income tax instead. This had first been introduced by Sir Robert Peel in 1844 as a temporary measure, but had not been introduced in Ireland.

By this decision of the new government, Ireland no longer had to repay the debt on the workhouses. The scheme had placed an enormous burden on the Irish people, and had given them 161 buildings, on a grand scale, which were the objects of fear and loathing on the part of the Irish people.

The Poor Laws had not led to the Prosperity and Happiness which Lord Russell had predicted. As Henry Grattan said

> If abandoned mansions, levelled cabins, bankrupt shopkeepers, ruined landlords, and starving people, were indications of prosperity, there might be some foundation for the statement of the noble Lord. A change had indeed taken place, and a fearful one, amongst the people—from plenty to scarcity; from great natural affection to intense selfishness; from charity to inhumanity… owing to the enactment of a law unsuited to the country, passed in defiance of her representatives, and continued in opposition to the declared opinions of every class of her people—a law which has not even answered the selfish objects of those who voted for it in this country, which has to be supported by 50,000 bayonets at an expense to the united empire of at least two millions annually.[136]

---

[134]House of Commons Debate, *Consolidated Annuities (Ireland)*. 07 April 1853.

[135] House of Commons Debate, *The Financial Statement-The Budget*. 19 April 1853. Paragraph 1403.

[136] House of Commons Debate, *Distressed-Unions-advances-and-repayment*. 15 February 1850.

The nightmare was over. The numbers in the workhouses increased for a few years, but from 1860 onwards the workhouses were never more than half full. In 1907 the Chancellor of the Exchequer H. H. Asquith introduced the Old Age Pension. Anybody who was 70 years or older got a basic pension of a shilling a week. This was enough to keep people out of the workhouse. In 1922, when the twenty six counties achieved their independence, the government of Michael Collins closed down the Irish workhouses. Since then they have been used for other purposes such as hospitals, or in many cases they have been knocked down.

The ones that are left stand as symbols of the injustices of the past.

The history of the Irish Famine is relevant today.

The bare bones of this story have been repeated often in history. It is a story of an economic cycle that is very relevant today. Bankers have money which they wish to invest. The best place to invest it is in a scheme which is guaranteed by a government. Just before the Irish famine, a scheme to build workhouses in Ireland and England seemed like a good scheme. 600 workhouses were built in England at this time. 161 workhouses were built in Ireland over a 13 year period. The loans for these workhouses had to be repaid. There were loans for the administration and maintenance of these workhouses which also had to be repaid.

Bankers regularly advance money for superstructure schemes such as dams, highways, prisons, national defence programmes, even wars, which all require the repayment of capital, and which are too big to challenge. At the first stage of this lending cycle there is a boom. People are employed. There is lots of optimism.

The second stage of this cycle is that the people have to be taxed heavily, in order to meet the repayments for these schemes. This stage often involves the moral admonishment of the poor taxpayers, who are blamed for not accepting responsibility for the money which has been loaned to them. The cartoon from Punch of the Englishman carrying the Irishman is a typical example. It expresses the view that those that can't pay their taxes are lazy and shirking their responsibilities. Austerity is the keyword in this phase.

The third stage of the cycle is that the people bearing the burden of repaying the taxes cannot do it. There is default and personnel misery for a lot of individuals, and in the Irish case, in the 1840's there was famine. The bankers and their associates move in and strip the assets of a country, acquiring them at a cheap rate.

The fourth phase of this cycle is the same as that which Lord Russell attempted to do in 1849, to offer easier terms of paying back the taxes. At first Russell offered a repayment period of 20 years, and then he extended it to 40 years.

The last phase of the cycle is that the bankers and their puppets "Drop the Debt".

The cycle of boom and bust that occurred in Ireland during the great famine was repeated again in the recent history of the Irish people, and of the Greek people. In the case of Greece, too much money was lent to the country by powerful banks. Amongst other loans, they received an advance of 53 billion euros to build an Olympic Stadium and all the surrounding services in 2005. When the repayment with interest was demanded back the people could not meet the amounts required. Two brave men tried to change the conditions for the people. They were Alexis Tsipras and Yanis Varoufakis. Just like William Smith O'Brien, they hoped to have the support of their people. Unfortunately they did not have the huge resources of the politicians in power in Europe. They achieved some things. At first their debt was rescheduled, from 20 years to 40 years (as Russell did for Ireland), interest rates were lowered, (as in the case of Ireland). Then, people were evicted, and homes were repossessed. Property and National assets were bought by foreign vulture funds at very low prices.

In the case of Ireland, the Irish banks took advantage of the very cheap loans which were offered by European banks. They offered loans to all and sundry in Ireland. There was no regulation from the Irish Government. Strictly speaking, the Irish Government was under no obligation to bail out the Irish banks, when the crash came. However there was extreme pressure put on them by the Troika of the European Central Bank, the European Commission, and the International Monetary Fund, to pay back the bad loans of the Irish Banks. The Government was faced with the threat that all the cash machines would be closed down if they did not agree. Unfortunately the Irish Government gave way to this pressure. The Troika also insisted that vulture funds should be allowed to buy up the bad loans at a very low price. These Vulture Funds are now creating unspeakable havoc on the ordinary Irish Citizen in extracting the money from them in a much shorter time than would normally be allowed for mortgage holders. They are also aggressively pursuing house owners through the courts and pressing for evictions. And strange to relate, the Irish Government passed into law an Act which banned the Irish from taking a class action against these Vulture Funds.

At the end of the Irish famine, a newly elected U.K. government forgave the debt. Together, with a little help from Rock Bands, from Bono and from Bob Geldof, it is time for us to serenade Europe and the elites and bankers of the world and ask them to "drop our debt." Soon, if the game continues as it has in the past, in the case of Greece and of Ireland, a new administration in Europe and worldwide will forgive the debt. And we can start all over again.

Or perhaps we will be more careful the next time round.

Appendices

Poor Laws Ireland

TO GEORGE NICHOLLS ESQ., &c&c&c

Whitehall, August 22nd, 1836

Sir,

In order to arrive at a practical conclusion with respect to any measures to be introduced into Parliament during the ensuing Session, for the benefit of the Poor in Ireland, it is most desirable, that a person well acquainted with the operation of the past and present system of the Poor Laws in England, should visit that part of the United Kingdom.

There is no one to whom I can entrust such a duty, more able to perform it with judgement and diligence, than yourself.

You will therefore, proceed to Ireland in the first week in September, taking with you the Report of the Commissioners of Poor Inquiry in Ireland.

The chief objects to which your attention need be directed are- that part of the Report which relates to the Relief of the Poor by Money payments, and the resource of Emigration.

You will examine how far it is judicious or practicable to offer relief to whole classes, whether of the Sick, the Infirm, or Orphan children.

You will consider whether such relief may not have the effect of promoting imposture, without destroying Mendicity; and whether the condition of the great bulk of the poorer classes will be improved by such a measure.

You will carefully weigh the important question-whether a rate, limited in amount rather than its application to particular classes, might be usefully directed to the erection and maintenance of Workhouses for all those who sought relief as Paupers. With a view to this question, you will inquire whether any kind of Workhouse can be established which shall not, in point of food clothing, and warmth, give its inmates a superior degree of comfort to the common lot of the independent labourer.

You will ask the opinion of experienced men, whether the restraint of a Workhouse would be an effectual check to applications for admission; and whether, if the system were once established, the inmates would not resist, by force the restraints which would be necessary.It

Supposing the Workhouse system not to be advisable, you will consider in what other mode a national or local rate might be beneficially applied.

You will examine the policy of establishing depots where candidates for Emigration might resort; and you will ascertain what method it is proposed to avoid the evil, said to be likely to flow from the establishment of Workhouses, and which might arise in like manner from the formation of depots for Emigration.

You will specially direct your attention to the machinery by which any rates for the relief of the Poor might be raised and expended; the formation and constitution of a Central Board, of Local Boards, of District Unions, and of Parochial Vestries.

Your attention need not be very specially given to the plans for the general improvement of Ireland, contained in the Report of the Commissioners of Inquiry: but you will generally remark upon those, or any other plans, which may lead to an increased demand for labour. You will also inquire whether, under the direction either of companies or individuals, the capital applied to the improvement of land, and reclaiming bogs and wastes, is perceptibly or notoriously increasing or diminishing.

You will also carefully read the Bills which have been brought into the House of Commons on this subject during the present year.

Lastly, I call your attention to the draft of a Bill prepared by one of the Commissioners of Inquiry, in conformity with their Report.

The Lord Lieutenant and Lord Morpeth will render you every assistance in their power,

I have the honour to be, Sir,

Your obedient servant,

J.RUSSELL.

This letter was the start of the project to build 161 workhouses in Ireland, at a cost of £ 1,200,000. Taxes were imposed on the people to pay for these workhouses, and this bankrupted the population. The letter was written by Lord Russell to George Nicholls on 22 August 1836. It is reproduced in the book "Three letters from George Nicholls to Lord Russell on the Poor Laws in Ireland".

Notes, Securities, Bullion, &c. of the Bank of England, as published Weekly in the *Gazette*, from the passing of the Act 7 & 8 Vict. c. 32, to the Week ending 24 April 1847.—*continued.*

| | ISSUE DEPARTMENT | | | | | BANKING DEPARTMENT | | | | | | | | |
WEEK ENDING	NOTES	Government Debt	Other Securities	BULLION — Gold	BULLION — Silver	CAPITAL	REST	DEPOSITS — Public	DEPOSITS — Private	DEPOSITS — Seven Days' and other Bills	SECURITIES — Public	SECURITIES — Other	NOTES	COIN
	£	£	£	£	£	£	£	£	£	£	£	£	£	£
1846:														
January 3	26,675,925	11,015,100	2,984,900	11,093,869	1,582,056	14,553,000	3,254,660	9,369,690	8,330,465	959,967	13,201,072	16,469,593	6,418,510	605,547
" 10	26,641,800	11,015,100	2,984,900	11,006,127	1,535,073	14,553,000	3,314,454	5,191,017	10,656,207	1,020,503	13,137,047	15,473,096	5,672,855	652,183
" 17	26,573,910	11,015,100	2,984,900	11,025,056	1,547,934	14,553,000	3,341,777	4,710,957	11,254,618	1,009,030	13,137,047	15,773,124	5,393,745	565,466
" 24	26,535,025	11,015,100	2,984,900	10,974,471	1,550,554	14,553,000	3,356,690	4,464,806	14,808,608	1,628,388	13,137,047	18,981,010	5,416,380	677,055
" 31	26,587,355	11,015,100	2,984,900	11,028,945	1,558,410	14,553,000	3,451,151	4,389,810	17,036,830	987,102	13,137,047	21,466,997	5,112,860	700,989
February 7	26,698,620	11,015,100	2,984,900	11,140,210	1,558,410	14,553,000	3,474,787	5,054,438	18,912,445	963,688	13,137,047	22,908,661	6,263,625	637,025
" 14	26,800,325	11,015,100	2,984,900	11,177,282	1,623,043	14,553,000	3,474,577	5,738,873	18,018,523	945,532	13,137,047	23,251,906	6,674,075	697,277
" 21	26,973,255	11,015,100	2,984,900	11,346,130	1,607,125	14,553,000	3,477,016	6,202,903	18,091,320	918,282	13,137,047	22,539,192	6,887,810	678,472
" 28	27,015,295	11,015,100	2,984,900	11,353,065	1,602,230	14,553,000	3,689,430	6,296,535	18,647,068	947,432	13,136,440	23,342,035	6,984,485	756,505
March 7	27,079,270	11,015,100	2,984,900	11,417,040	1,602,239	14,553,000	3,757,708	6,592,355	17,868,778	898,176	13,136,440	24,118,987	7,576,625	707,965
" 14	27,117,805	11,015,100	2,984,900	11,407,534	1,710,281	14,553,000	3,767,623	6,804,524	17,476,098	887,487	13,136,440	21,923,787	7,712,120	717,285
" 21	27,264,475	11,015,100	2,984,900	11,554,194	1,710,281	14,553,000	3,780,009	7,065,422	17,356,203	881,887	13,136,440	21,806,194	8,093,665	700,222
" 28	27,269,245	11,015,100	2,984,900	11,558,984	1,710,281	14,553,000	3,789,071	7,319,625	17,103,928	953,579	13,136,731	22,181,392	7,683,690	718,490
April 4	27,181,080	11,015,100	2,984,900	11,460,445	1,721,535	14,553,000	3,799,508	7,074,026	16,763,047	965,446	13,136,440	22,058,631	7,316,415	643,541
" 11	27,030,355	11,015,100	2,984,900	11,308,300	1,721,955	14,553,000	3,352,291	4,210,976	18,069,093	959,379	14,437,065	19,438,782	6,728,120	544,772
" 18	27,031,510	11,015,100	2,984,900	11,250,593	1,780,017	14,553,000	3,359,084	3,197,029	17,710,087	986,017	13,957,865	18,736,602	6,515,990	595,660
" 25	27,049,510	11,015,100	2,984,900	11,256,880	1,794,630	14,553,000	3,364,576	3,698,953	16,978,110	962,415	13,578,065	17,584,532	6,488,140	656,317
May 2	27,072,295	11,015,100	2,984,900	11,279,130	1,793,165	14,553,000	3,396,540	2,578,451	16,786,380	965,730	13,393,665	17,991,148	6,408,470	661,418
" 9	27,044,995	11,015,100	2,984,900	11,451,830	1,793,165	14,553,000	3,406,284	3,031,375	16,256,526	981,417	13,023,065	17,734,025	6,836,405	635,107
" 16	27,520,215	11,015,100	2,984,900	11,623,619	1,886,596	14,553,000	3,418,372	4,084,117	16,354,017	963,128	12,988,065	18,221,548	7,497,460	664,461
" 23	27,706,865	11,015,100	2,984,900	11,782,453	1,944,412	14,553,000	3,426,036	4,809,183	15,947,268	970,461	12,988,665	18,226,480	7,774,025	706,478
" 30	27,993,880	11,015,100	2,984,900	12,062,597	1,931,283	14,553,000	3,378,878	5,228,640	16,105,620	899,192	13,008,065	18,460,493	8,043,560	704,212
June 6	28,335,000	11,015,100	2,984,900	12,194,710	2,132,250	14,553,000	3,379,044	5,753,512	15,997,013	852,008	12,988,665	18,321,641	8,468,180	686,091
" 13	28,563,335	11,015,100	2,984,900	12,371,105	2,232,290	14,553,000	3,386,810	6,537,132	15,518,397	862,605	12,988,065	18,122,098	9,011,510	736,331
" 20	29,005,160	11,015,100	2,984,900	12,592,403	2,412,757	14,553,000	3,396,774	7,313,539	15,203,009	832,981	13,000,046	17,984,603	9,631,235	683,419
" 27	29,273,165	11,015,100	2,984,900	12,849,579	2,443,536	14,553,000	3,405,354	7,807,802	15,034,361	851,222	12,987,046	18,257,149	9,664,090	744,554
July 4	29,322,400	11,015,100	2,984,900	12,995,074	2,417,126	14,553,000	3,424,178	7,794,200	14,402,460	887,364	12,987,142	18,145,319	9,393,090	625,651
" 11	29,266,360	11,015,100	2,984,900	12,844,442	2,421,918	14,553,000	3,482,541	3,489,416	15,661,286	941,566	12,962,147	16,143,726	8,435,630	596,366
" 18	29,139,905	11,015,100	2,984,900	12,703,542	2,436,263	14,553,000	3,504,138	3,162,696	14,994,973	989,462	12,961,560	15,382,397	8,139,020	630,492
" 25	29,313,945	11,015,100	2,984,900	12,875,243	2,437,702	14,553,000	3,508,378	3,438,401	14,305,341	920,016	12,961,735	14,683,407	8,362,695	639,482
August 1	29,292,320	11,015,100	2,984,900	12,854,618	2,437,700	14,553,000	3,697,079	3,793,610	13,449,388	943,443	12,961,735	14,661,735	8,796,875	510,233
" 8	29,386,305	11,015,100	2,984,900	12,635,426	2,430,879	14,553,000	3,603,683	5,014,200	12,456,737	957,056	12,961,735	13,684,578	9,075,160	558,203
" 15	29,456,535	11,015,100	2,984,900	12,923,912	2,427,693	14,553,000	3,611,498	6,135,636	10,794,573	905,994	12,961,735	13,848,441	8,861,335	388,960
" 22	29,653,990	11,015,100	2,984,900	13,143,719	2,508,471	14,553,000	3,613,216	6,843,002	10,074,046	920,016	12,961,735	13,012,824	8,206,625	392,256
" 29	29,875,890	11,015,100	2,984,900	13,190,102	2,576,788	14,553,000	3,554,370	7,142,919	9,161,368	888,580	12,961,735	12,395,457	9,449,760	495,178

Appendix 2 The Bank of England was becoming bankrupt in 1846-1847. These extracts from Parliamentary papers show how the gold held in the vaults of the Bank of England was being sent abroad from September 1846 to April 1847. In September 1846 there was £13,057,997 worth of gold in the vaults, in April 1847 there was £7,120,006. *(column 4 next page).* Parliamentary Papers, 1847 (360) *Bank of England.- Bank notes. A return of the notes, securities, bullion, &c., of the Bank of England, as published in the Gazette.* Page image 2 of 6.
Image courtesy of the National Library of Ireland.

September	5	29,760,870	11,015,100	2,084,900	13,057,997	2,702,873	14,553,000	3,864,479	935,830	8,557,109	7,318,919	12,261,735	12,522,550	9,231,995	512,957
"	12	29,804,060	11,015,100	2,084,900	13,154,883	2,710,077	14,553,000	3,861,789	993,872	8,095,203	8,198,800	12,261,350	12,321,816	9,846,600	488,888
"	19	29,758,615	11,015,100	2,084,900	13,044,770	2,713,845	14,553,000	3,873,491	869,247	8,316,924	8,765,570	12,261,350	13,049,901	9,817,195	550,676
"	26	29,655,855	11,015,100	2,084,900	12,930,614	2,725,241	14,553,000	3,878,988	995,955	8,260,779	9,755,977	12,261,350	14,036,157	9,788,685	568,497
October	3	29,359,795	11,015,100	2,084,900	12,632,704	2,727,001	14,553,000	3,886,985	930,793	8,167,143	9,776,195	12,61,350	15,686,775	8,869,150	456,681
"	10	29,078,135	11,015,100	2,084,900	12,400,634	2,677,501	14,553,000	3,383,158	938,723	8,322,626	9,801,402	12,61,350	15,227,665	8,305,785	504,609
"	17	28,741,645	11,015,100	2,084,900	12,192,882	2,618,763	14,553,000	3,434,339	982,438	9,084,274	5,356,260	12,808,119	14,788,639	7,499,870	401,403
"	24	28,437,345	11,015,100	2,084,900	11,868,690	2,568,555	14,553,000	3,435,671	1,026,996	8,755,441	4,890,737	12,808,119	12,319,710	7,157,355	456,661
"	31	28,309,895	11,015,100	2,084,900	11,793,084	2,516,811	14,553,000	3,463,463	1,016,015	8,751,736	4,632,177	12,808,119	12,175,968	6,934,120	498,184
November	7	28,235,885	11,015,100	2,084,900	11,724,111	2,511,774	14,553,000	3,468,352	1,018,610	8,281,624	5,428,783	12,808,119	12,153,009	7,264,620	524,621
"	14	28,246,995	11,015,100	2,084,900	11,739,837	2,596,458	14,553,000	3,474,506	972,112	7,995,492	6,777,777	12,808,119	12,325,905	7,836,335	602,458
"	21	28,317,840	11,015,100	2,084,900	11,811,382	2,596,458	14,553,000	3,484,689	990,484	7,075,058	7,876,390	12,808,119	13,353,075	8,109,895	605,032
"	28	28,313,545	11,015,100	2,084,900	11,807,087	2,596,458	14,553,000	3,479,967	892,355	8,018,391	8,447,560	12,808,119	13,562,822	8,395,745	694,587
December	5	28,269,105	11,015,100	2,084,900	11,762,647	2,596,458	14,553,000	3,434,203	895,483	8,303,593	8,612,488	12,807,417	13,353,212	8,402,300	733,768
"	12	28,410,735	11,015,100	2,084,900	11,935,818	2,474,917	14,553,000	3,437,378	886,995	7,991,126	9,185,471	12,807,417	13,879,060	8,643,815	742,778
"	19	28,413,000	11,015,100	2,084,900	11,943,510	2,489,490	14,553,000	3,440,384	868,439	7,615,703	9,847,743	12,807,417	13,904,284	8,884,445	749,663
"	26	28,449,630	11,015,100	2,084,900	11,972,540	2,489,490	14,553,000	3,447,406	881,528	7,696,172	10,341,314	12,847,179	14,654,995	8,813,675	624,661
1847:															
January	2	28,958,260	11,015,100	2,084,900	11,788,770	2,469,490	14,553,000	3,469,857	901,139	7,903,050	9,990,664	12,896,362	15,071,820	8,327,085	693,312
"	9	27,552,100	11,015,100	2,084,900	11,482,442	2,069,658	14,553,000	3,520,048	975,005	9,784,767	5,860,631	12,757,326	14,404,948	6,715,255	755,922
"	16	27,925,335	11,015,100	2,084,900	11,356,608	1,808,667	14,553,000	3,551,483	598,959	10,339,726	5,034,189	12,757,326	14,453,711	6,545,065	733,346
"	23	26,766,260	11,015,100	2,084,900	11,091,751	1,674,599	14,553,000	3,560,665	952,784	10,355,835	4,668,489	12,757,326	14,489,657	6,167,170	676,620
"	30	26,172,870	11,015,100	2,084,900	10,499,161	1,673,799	14,553,000	3,643,741	941,481	9,659,940	4,463,872	12,725,619	14,106,072	5,703,555	728,788
February	6	25,504,335	11,015,100	2,084,900	9,963,744	1,540,581	14,553,000	3,650,686	952,689	9,182,765	4,668,298	12,313,175	14,019,036	5,890,855	789,412
"	13	25,471,205	11,015,100	2,084,900	9,930,684	1,540,581	14,553,000	3,671,499	895,352	9,320,852	5,298,594	12,161,087	15,071,256	5,747,330	827,844
"	20	25,458,405	11,015,100	2,084,900	9,922,816	1,535,649	14,553,000	3,663,132	820,491	8,837,993	5,869,323	11,999,079	15,039,339	5,076,535	756,296
"	27	25,349,820	11,015,100	2,084,900	9,801,418	1,548,392	14,553,000	3,899,220	818,634	9,321,695	5,928,487	11,999,079	15,819,148	6,016,695	695,114
March	6	24,993,385	11,015,100	2,084,900	9,445,403	1,548,392	14,553,000	3,951,922	846,860	9,288,661	6,571,731	11,999,079	16,905,705	5,714,740	601,650
"	13	24,786,340	11,015,100	2,084,900	9,237,948	1,548,392	14,553,000	3,942,288	798,465	9,536,137	6,716,162	11,999,079	17,358,712	5,554,140	663,121
"	20	24,487,035	11,015,100	2,084,900	8,963,070	1,533,965	14,553,000	3,971,704	844,630	9,062,436	6,471,623	11,999,079	17,650,874	5,418,745	743,695
"	27	24,236,340	11,015,100	2,084,900	8,820,737	1,469,603	14,553,000	3,978,633	834,640	9,403,132	6,616,487	11,999,079	17,834,355	4,876,015	695,243
April	3	23,554,640	11,015,100	2,084,900	8,066,355	1,488,285	14,553,000	3,901,333	960,294	9,502,091	6,001,947	11,999,079	18,627,116	3,699,700	691,770
"	10	23,339,340	11,015,100	2,084,900	7,795,044	1,440,696	14,553,000	3,391,768	987,562	11,357,744	4,084,375	13,574,444	18,136,377	2,833,915	690,713
"	17	22,801,100	11,015,100	2,084,900	7,305,424	1,435,676	14,553,000	3,307,077	910,068	10,004,699	3,011,932	11,677,819	17,111,001	2,558,315	538,741
"	24	22,549,140	11,015,100	2,084,900	7,180,066	1,459,134	14,553,000	3,400,789	866,975	9,125,409	2,634,518	11,117,319	16,079,697	2,718,995	604,750

B

(No. 2.)

Bank of England,
4 May 1847.

M. Marshall,
Chief Cashier.

Appendix 3. The Bank of England could only issue paper currency to the value of £14,000,000 above the gold which they held in the vaults. This gold was flowing out to America because speculators were buying wheat, hoping to ma[ke] a profit when the Corn Laws were repealed. This speculation almost caused the Bank of England to collapse. It mad[e] things more difficult for the Irish, as the government had no money to give them as grants for food.

Image courtesy of the National Library of Ireland.

Appendix 4. This is a copy of a page from the Report of the Boundary Commissioners in 1849. It gives the names of all the workhouses which have been built between the years 1840 and 1845. It was a massive building programme which took place in a short five years, and which cost £1,200,000 at that time, which would be billions in today's money. The report also names the places where it was proposed that another 50 workhouse should be built. Only thirty of these were actually built, between 1849 and 1853.

Poor Law Boundary Commission   Table   Present Unions

. Abbeyleix.	27. Carrick-on Suir.	53. Dunmanway.	79. Limerick.	105. Newtownards.
. Antrim.	28. Cashel.	54. Dunshaughlin.	80. Lisbourne.	106. Newtown Limavaddy
. Ardee.	29. Castlebar.	55. Edenderry.	81. Lismore.	107. Oldcastle.
. Armagh.	30. Castleblaney.	56. Ennis.	82. Lismore.	108. Omagh.
. Athlone.	31. Castlederg.	57. Enniscorthy.	83. Listowel.	109. Parsonstown.
. Athy.	32. Castlerea.	58. Enniskillen.	84. Londonderry.	110. Rathdown.
. Bailieborough.	33. Cavan.	59. Ennistymon.	85. Longford.	111. Rathdrum.
. Ballina.	34. Celbridge.	60. Fermoy.	86. Loughrea.	112. Rathkeale.
. Ballinasloe.	35. Clifdon.	61. Galway.	87. Lowtherstown	113. Roscommon.
0. Ballinrobe.	36. Clogheen.	62. Glenties.	88. Lurgan.	114. Roscrea.
1. Ballycastle.	37. Clogher.	63. Gorey.	89. Macroom	115. Scariff.
2. Ballymena.	38. Clones.	64. Gort.	90. Magherafelt.	116. Shillelagh.
3. Ballymoney.	39. Clonmel.	65. Gortin.	91. Mallow.	117. Skibbereen.
4. Ballyshannon.	40. Coleraine.	66. Granard.	92. Manorhamilton.	118. Sligo.
5. Balrothery.	41. Cookstown.	67. Inishowen.	93. Middleton.	119. Strabane.
6. Baltingglass.	42. Cootehill.	68. Kanturk.	94. Milford.	120. Stranolar.
7. Banbridge.	43. Cork.	69. Kells.	95. Mohill.	121. Swineford.
8. Bandon.	44. Donegal.	70. Kenmare.	96. Monaghan.	122. Thurles.
9. Bantry.	45. Downpatrick.	71. Kileel.	97. Mountmellick.	123. Tipperary.
0. Belfast.	46. Drogheda.	72. Kilkenny.	98. Mullingar.	124. Tralee.
1. Boyle.	47. Dublin, North.	73. Killarney.	99. Naas.	125. Trim.
2. Cahieciveen.	48. Dublin, South.	74. Kilmallock.	100. Navan.	126. Tuam.
3. Callan.	49. Dundalk.	75. Kilrush.	101. Nenagh.	127. Tullamore.
4. Carlow.	50. Dunfanaghy.	76. Kinsale.	102. Newcastle.	128. Waterford.
5. Carrickmacross.	51. Dungannon.	77. Larne.	103. New Ross.	129. Westport.
6. Carrick-on-Shannon.	52. Dungarvan.	78. Letterkenny.	104. Newry.	130. Wexford.
Dingle.				

Proposed Unions, *Arranged in the order in which they are most urgently required.*

. Belmullet.	11. Drumkeeran.	21. Mount Bellow.	31. Cussane.	41. North Cork.
. Ballycastle, or Killala.	12. Cappamore.	22. Castle Island.	32. Riverstown, or Ballymote.	42. Glin.
. Dromore West.	13. Bawnboy.	23. Urlingford.	33. Portumna.	43. Kildysart.
. Castletown Berehaven	14. Arvagh.	24. Millstreet.	34 Tulla.	44. Croom.
. Clonakilty.	15. Youghal.	25. Thomastown.	35. Corrofin.	45. Castletown Delvin.
. Skull.	16. Mitchelstown.	26. Ballymore.	36. Ballyvaughan.	46. Donaghmore.
. Newport.	17. Claremorris.	27. Castlecomer.	37. Ferbane.	47. Mountrath.
. Oughterard.	18. Strokestown.	28. Kilorglin.	38. Ballymahon.	48. Newtown Mount Kennedy.
. Killybegs.	19. Glenamadda.	29. Kiledmond.	39. Borrisokane.	49. Blessington.
0. Tubbercurry.	20. Milford.	30. Kilmacthomas.	40. Kildare.	50. Kilrea.

Return of Passenger Ships arrived at the Port of Quebec in the Season of 1847, &c.—*continued.*

Date of Arrival at Quebec.	Vessel's Name.	Whence.	Length of Passage to Quarantine, in Days.	Detention in Quarantine, in Days.	Souls Embarked.		Deaths.			Total Deaths.
							On Board.		In Quarantine Hospital.	
					Cabin.	Steerage.	On the Passage.	At Quarantine.		
9 Sept.	Highland Mary	Cork	48	3	..	100	4	1	2	7
10 Sept.	Maria Somes	,,	32	18	..	329	17	..	32	49
12 Sept.	Belleisle	Glasgow	31	..	7	21	..	..	..	..
,,	Spermaceti	Plymouth	40	..	5	197	..	..	..	..
,,	John Bull	London	28	..	..	23	..	..	..	..
,,	General Hewitt	Bremen	52	..	..	516	12	..	..	12
,,	Atalanta	Dublin	44	..	..	226	4	1	..	5
,,	Erromanga	Glasgow	35	..	20	36	..	..	..	..
,,	Tottenham	New Ross	37	..	..	5	..	..	..	..
,,	Great Britain	London	..	..	..	13	..	..	..	..
,,	Mersey	Torquay	39	..	..	8	..	..	..	..
14 Sept.	George Ramsay	New Ross	53	..	..	26	..	..	..	..
17 Sept.	Superior	Londonderry	51	10	..	366	18	8	13	39
,,	Jane Black	Limerick	33	3	..	395	2	2	..	4
,,	Eliza	Glasgow	54	8	..	269	29	..	16	45
,,	Emerald	Newry	40	1	..	85	1	..	..	1
,,	Charles	Youghal	40	1	..	65	..	..	..	..
,,	Isabella	Killala	57	5	..	236	8	..	4	12
19 Sept.	Sir Robert Peel	Liverpool	51	4	..	480	31	2	16	49
,,	Pearl	London	34	.	..	12	..	..	..	..
,,	Argyll	Newport	40	5	2	362	5	..	7	12
20 Sept.	Wellington	Liverpool	46	7	1	438	26	..	5	31
,,	Virgilia	,,	54	6	..	208	12	..	5	17
24 Sept.	Cherokee	Glasgow	41	..	5	..	..	..	..	..
,,	Florence	Plymouth	35	..	..	11	..	..	..	..
25 Sept.	Emperor	,,	35	..	..	5	..	..	..	..
,,	Sophia	Waterford	42	6	..	23	..	..	..	..
,,	Chieftain	Belfast	46	..	1	95	..	..	..	..
,,	Gentoo	Plymouth	37	1	3	49	..	..	..	..
,,	Victoria	St. Ives	45	1	..	44	..	..	..	..
,,	Ariel	Kilrush	47	..	..	119	..	..	..	..
,,	Anne	Limerick	39	7	..	116	..	..	..	..
,,	Florence	Cardiff	..	..	..	1	..	..	..	..
27 Sept.	Nerio	Limerick	48	5	..	134	3	..	..	3
29 Sept.	Henrietta Mary	Cork	37	4	1	266	12	..	7	19
,,	Albion	,,	45	3	1	183	5	..	1	6
30 Sept.	Douce Davie	Sligo	44	6	7	274	6	..	1	7
3 Oct.	Favourite	Greenock	43	..	3	16	..	..	..	..
,,	Emigrant	Liverpool	50	3	1	528	43	2	40	85
6 Oct.	Douglas	London	42	..	..	20	..	..	..	..
7 Oct.	Sir Colin Campbell	Belfast	42	..	4	381	2	..	..	2
8 Oct.	Constance	Bristol	46	..	..	9	..	..	..	..
,,	Mary	Glasgow	47	..	..	20	..	..	..	..
9 Oct.	Peruvian	,,	..	..	..	1	..	..	..	..
,,	Sarah Milledge	Galway	52	3	11	259	5	..	3	8
10 Oct.	Earl Powis	Dundee	52	..	8	12	..	..	..	..
,,	Lord Metcalfe	Aberdeen	52	..	15	36	..	..	..	..
12 Oct.	John Hawkes	Limerick	48	1	3	111	5	..	..	5
13 Oct.	Bryan Abbs	,,	61	..	..	179	5	..	..	5
,,	H. Lawrence	Aberdeen	46	..	3	23	..	..	..	..
14 Oct.	Messenger	Liverpool	49	2	..	227	12	..	1	13
15 Oct.	Clio	Padstow	51	..	1	208	..	..	..	..
,,	Ninian	Limerick	45	1	10	99	1	..	..	1
1 Nov.	Lord Ashburton	Liverpool	47	2	2	481	65	..	..	65
4 Nov.	Douglas	Hull	87	..	..	10	..	..	..	..
8 Nov.	Richard Watson	Sligo	42	..	1	169	4	..	..	4
						97,628				
Total Arrived of Shipwrecked Passengers					..	325				
Totals					696	97,953	4,092	1,190	3,389	8,671

Appendix 5. This page is part of a Parliamentary Report on Emigration to Canada in 1847. It gives the number of people who died, either through drowning or through fever during that time. Most of the deaths were on ships which came from Irish ports. Total deaths in 1847 were 8,671 people.

1847-48 (932) (964) (971) (985) *Papers relative to emigration to the British Provinces in North America. (in continuation of the Papers presented December 1947)* Page image 101 of 154.

Image courtesy of the National Library of Ireland.

Kilrush Union.

of these hovels defies description. I, not long since, found a widow whose three children were in fever, occupying the piggery of their former cabin, which lay beside them in ruins; however incredible it may appear, this place where they had lived for weeks, measured 5 feet by 4 feet, and of corresponding height. I offered her a free conveyance to the workhouse, which she steadily refused; her piggery was knocked down as soon as her children were able to crawl out on recovery: and she has now gone forth a wanderer. I could not induce any neighbour to take her in, even for payment; she had medical aid, and all necessary relief from the Union.

There are considerable numbers in this Union at present houseless, or still worse, living in places unfit for human habitation where disease will be constantly generated.

The workhouse has been frequently swamped by this class, and the hospital and infirmary must be so while such a state of things exists.

I would not presume to meddle with the rights of property, nor yet to argue the expediency or necessity of these "monster clearances," both one and the other no doubt frequently exist; this, however, renders the efficient and systematic administration of the Poor Law no less difficult and embarrassing. I think it incumbent on me to state these facts for the Commissioners' information that they may be aware of some of the difficulties I have to deal with.

The difficulty of arriving at strictly accurate information on this head, is obvious; but the general accuracy of the returns I forward may be relied upon. They show the name of the lands and the numbers evicted, being 2,801 persons. I have returns of about 400 more in preparation, and I do not think I have yet got through two-thirds of the number of houses levelled or persons evicted in the Union. A great number of temporary huts which have been erected are altogether insufficient for shelter in the winter months. The listless and improvident owners lack the means and energy to better them.

ENCLOSURES.

LIST of Names and Number of FAMILIES Evicted and driven from the Lands of Clohanes, Rhineagonnought, and Doonbey, Parish of Killard, the Property of Stackpooles, Minors, all within the last Three Months.

No.	Heads of Families.	No. in Family	Males.	Fem.	How dis-possessed.	Cause.	Title.	Quantity of Land in Holding.	Yearly Rent.	Arrears.	Observations.
									£. s. d.		
1	Widow Markhain	6	3	3	Evicted.	Non-payment.	At will.	3½ acres	3 10 0	..	House thrown down, getting out-door relief.
2	Michael M'Namara	2	1	1	,,	,,	,,	House	0 17 6	..	
3	Connor Killeen	5	3	2	,,	,,	,,	1½ acres	1 15 0	..	,, ,,
4	John Stackpoole	2	1	1	,,	,,	,,	1½ ,,	1 15 0	..	,, ,,
5	Widow Considine	4	2	2	,,	..	,,	House	..	..	Work-rent, house thrown down, getting out-door relief.
6	John Casey	6	4	2	,,	Non-payment.	,,	1 acre	1 3 1	..	House thrown down, getting out-door relief.
7	Widow Casey	2	..	2	,,	,,	,,	1 ,,	2 0 0	..	,, turned out by Dr. Shannon, middleman.
8	John Doyle, sen.	11	4	7	,,	,,	,,	6 acres	5 0 0	..	House thrown down.
9	John Doyle, jun.	4	3	1	,,	Non-payment.	,,	6 ,,	4 10 0	..	,,
10	Widow M'Namara	5	3	2	,,	,,	,,	6 ,,	4 10 0	..	
11	Widow Doyle	3	1	2	,,	..	,,	House	..	..	Work-rent, house thrown down.
12	Tim Gorman	6	3	3	,,	..	,,	,,	..	..	,, ,,
13	Michael Corry	3	1	2	,,	..	,,	,,	..	..	,, ,,
14	John Carmody	7	4	3	,,	..	,,	,,	..	..	,, ,,
15	John Ryan	3	1	2	,,	Non-payment.	,,	1 acre	1 10 0	..	House thrown down.
16	Pat Ryan	6	4	2	,,	,,	,,	2 acres	1 10 0	..	
17	Pat White	3	2	1	,,	..	,,	House	..	..	
18	Charles Brady	2	1	1	,,	..	,,	,,	..	..	Work-rent, house thrown down.
19	Richard Harvey	7	3	4	,,	Non-payment.	,,	,,	..	..	,, ,,
20	Michael Halloran	3	2	1	,,	,,	,,	½ acre	0 15 4	..	House thrown down by Dr. Shannon.
21	Pat Crowley	7	3	4	,,	,,	,,	2 acres	3 1 6	..	House thrown down.
22	Martin Halloran	9	4	5	,,	,,	,,	1 acre	1 11 6	..	,, ,,
23	Michael Lynch	6	3	3	,,	,,	,,	House	1 0 0	..	,, ,,
24	Pat Toole	7	6	1	,,	Non-payment.	,,	,,	1 0 0	..	Work-rent; house thrown down.
25	Connor M'Namara	2	1	1	,,	..	,,	,,	1 0 0	..	House thrown down.
26	Edmond Ryan	7	4	3	,,	..	,,	,,	1 0 0	..	,,
27	Michael Cusack	6	4	2	,,	..	,,	,,	1 0 0	..	,,
28	John Haugh	4	2	2	,,	..	,,	,,	1 0 0	..	,,
29	Widow Lynch	6	3	3	,,	..	,,	6 acres	12 0 0	..	
30	Edmond Eustace	6	4	2	,,	..	,,	House	1 0 0	..	
31	Tom M'Mahon	9	3	6	,,	..	Non title.	,,	1 0 0	..	House thrown down, and getting relief.

Appendix 6. This is a page from a Parliamentary Report on evictions in the Kilrush Union in 1849. The Report was from Captain Kennedy, the Temporary Relieving Officer. He said "I do not presume to meddle in the rights of property" but "I feel it incumbent on me to state these facts." The Poor Law Commissioners wrote that they did not require him to send any more lists of names of those who were evicted.

Parliamentary Papers, 1849 (177) Reports and returns relating to evictions in the Kilrush Union. Page image 8 of 58. Image courtesy of the National Library of Ireland.

SUMMARY of WEEKLY RETURNS of PAUPERS in the Union Workhouses in Ireland, from the 4th of April, 1846, to 10th of April, 1847, both inclusive; distinguishing the several Classes, the Number of Sick and Lunatic Paupers, and the Number of Deaths during each Week; showing also the Number of Paupers in the Union Workhouses at the close of each corresponding Week in the preceding Year.

Week ended Saturday,	No. of Workhouses open		Number of Paupers in the Workhouses at the close of the Weeks ended as set forth in the first Column.						No. of Paupers in Workhouses, at the close of the corresponding Week in the preceding Year.	Sick, and Lunatic, and Idiot Paupers, (included in preceding Classes) Inmates at the close of the Weeks ended as set forth in first Column.				Increase on each Week as compared with corresponding Week in preceding Year.	Total Deaths during the Week.	Weekly Rate of Mortality per 1000.
	In 1846-7	In 1845-6	Males aged 15 and upwards.	Females aged 15 and upwards.	Boys under 15.	Girls under 15.	Children under 2.	Total No. of Inmates on the above date.		Sick.			Lunatics and Idiots.			
										In General Hospital.	In Fever Hospital.	Total Sick.				
1846																
4 April	123	117	9,751	15,598	12,069	10,579	2,864	50,861	41,651	7,257	864	8,121	1,313	9,210	159	3·
11 „	124	117	9,675	15,442	12,026	10,542	2,846	50,531	40,788	7,208	858	8,066	1,265	9,743	222	4·
18 „	124	117	9,659	15,394	12,110	10,647	2,865	50,675	40,240	7,200	831	8,031	1,321	10,435	211	4·
25 „	125	118	9,559	15,400	12,124	10,698	2,869	50,650	39,538	7,222	844	8,066	1,334	11,112	275	5·4
2 May	125	118	9,487	15,270	12,113	10,667	2,823	50,360	39,480	7,230	836	8,066	1,328	10,880	224	4·5
9 „	126	118	9,498	15,284	12,173	10,720	2,847	50,522	39,141	7,191	886	8,077	1,325	11,381	164	3·2
16 „	126	118	9,571	15,380	12,268	10,745	2,877	50,841	38,848	7,158	954	8,112	1,341	11,993	209	4·
23 „	126	118	9,657	15,464	12,351	10,843	2,922	51,237	38,598	7,223	1,016	8,239	1,348	12,639	208	4·
30 „	126	118	9,590	15,485	12,311	10,896	2,921	51,203	38,599	6,781	1,075	7,856	1,342	12,604	191	3·7
6 June	127	118	9,632	15,499	12,232	10,944	2,939	51,246	38,775	6,644	1,147	7,791	1,345	12,471	192	3·7
13 „	127	118	9,649	15,485	12,266	10,932	2,970	51,302	38,876	6,581	1,155	7,736	1,310	12,426	163	3·1
20 „	127	118	9,621	15,408	12,227	10,954	2,938	51,148	38,882	6,345	1,167	7,512	1,347	12,266	165	3·2
27 „	127	119	9,531	15,341	12,126	10,849	2,914	50,761	38,815	6,482	1,181	7,663	1,350	11,946	154	3·
4 July	127	119	9,665	15,214	12,088	10,806	2,923	50,696	38,753	6,338	1,262	7,600	1,360	11,943	146	2·9
11 „	127	119	9,517	15,145	12,067	10,762	2,878	50,369	38,860	6,322	1,161	7,483	1,350	11,509	162	3·2
18 „	127	119	9,494	15,118	12,011	10,763	2,894	50,280	38,945	6,189	1,145	7,334	1,366	11,335	153	3·
25 „	127	119	9,367	14,969	11,877	10,683	2,852	49,748	38,950	6,129	1,083	7,212	1,352	10,798	154	3·
1 Aug.	128	119	9,153	14,750	11,720	10,541	2,814	48,978	38,933	5,964	1,072	7,036	1,377	10,045	160	3·3
8 „	128	119	8,697	13,981	11,159	10,070	2,624	46,531	38,617	5,914	964	6,878	1,334	7,914	130	2·8
15 „	128	119	8,403	13,275	10,708	9,654	2,407	44,447	37,914	5,902	965	6,867	1,337	6,533	137	3·
22 „	128	119	8,268	13,113	10,629	9,507	2,409	43,866	37,231	5,774	932	6,706	1,363	6,635	158	3·6
29 „	128	119	8,208	13,037	10,584	9,462	2,364	43,655	35,801	5,662	876	6,538	1,362	7,854	155	3·6
5 Sept.	128	119	8,388	13,208	10,701	9,613	2,381	44,291	34,792	5,720	874	6,594	1,380	9,499	122	2·7
12 „	128	119	8,627	13,548	11,003	9,887	2,492	45,547	34,197	5,691	817	6,508	1,377	11,350	134	2·9
19 „	128	119	8,873	13,977	11,362	10,205	2,603	47,020	33,998	5,791	815	6,606	1,379	13,022	145	3·
26 „	128	119	9,263	14,551	11,878	10,711	2,765	49,168	33,835	5,911	849	6,760	1,384	15,333	134	2·7
3 Oct.	128	120	9,574	15,255	12,548	11,236	2,930	51,543	33,933	6,057	886	6,943	1,398	17,605	163	3·2
10 „	128	120	10,070	16,314	13,544	12,157	3,208	55,293	34,000	6,248	910	7,158	1,389	21,203	183	3·3
17 „	129	120	10,668	17,480	14,677	13,216	3,555	59,596	34,322	6,591	934	7,525	1,420	25,274	205	3·4
24 „	129	121	11,264	18,815	15,886	14,278	3,936	64,179	34,400	6,832	969	7,801	1,437	29,779	241	3·7
31 „	129	121	11,718	20,077	17,202	15,540	4,302	68,839	34,564	7,264	1,038	8,302	1,456	34,275	277	4·
7 Nov.	129	122	12,440	21,632	18,565	16,863	4,675	74,175	35,009	7,380	1,279	8,659	1,503	39,166	312	4·2
14 „	129	122	12,663	22,510	19,179	17,523	4,800	76,675	35,711	8,024	1,351	9,375	1,474	40,964	364	4·7
21 „	129	122	13,091	23,725	20,268	18,520	5,038	80,642	36,802	8,572	1,438	10,010	1,508	43,840	454	5·6
28 „	129	122	13,501	24,856	21,161	19,417	5,190	84,125	37,934	9,654	1,530	11,184	1,529	46,171	409	5·9
5 Dec.	129	123	14,081	26,344	22,253	20,473	5,452	88,603	39,110	10,505	1,823	12,328	1,538	49,493	662	7·4
12 „	129	123	14,384	27,431	23,114	21,408	5,616	91,953	40,249	10,942	1,796	12,738	1,556	51,704	791	8·6
19 „	129	123	15,065	28,657	24,103	22,427	5,908	96,061	41,104	11,604	2,063	13,667	1,576	54,957	989	10·3
26 „	129	123	15,007	28,745	24,198	22,598	5,700	96,248	41,214	12,273	2,198	14,471	1,592	54,034	1,054	11·
1847.																
2 Jan.	129	123	15,307	29,654	24,835	23,180	5,786	98,762	42,645	12,841	2,560	15,401	1,678	56,117	1,206	12·2
9 „	129	123	15,616	30,930	25,504	23,904	5,935	101,889	43,764	13,468	2,922	16,390	1,645	58,125	1,257	12·3
16 „	129	123	16,099	32,387	26,393	24,990	6,115	105,984	44,990	14,195	3,365	17,560	1,696	60,994	1,279	12·
23 „	129	123	16,375	33,238	26,993	25,719	6,158	108,483	46,662	14,671	3,942	18,613	1,696	61,821	1,405	13·
30 „	129	123	16,603	34,426	27,706	26,607	6,279	111,621	47,256	15,112	4,358	19,470	1,635	64,365	1,493	13·3
6 Feb.	129	123	16,668	35,054	28,119	26,977	6,148	112,966	47,569	16,339	4,902	21,241	1,673	64,997	1,915	17·
13 „	129	123	16,949	35,643	28,413	27,285	6,108	114,398	48,436	15,979	5,541	21,520	1,655	65,962	2,178	19·
20 „	129	123	17,186	36,084	28,817	27,658	6,037	115,782	48,463	16,503	6,177	22,680	1,636	67,319	2,133	18·4
27 „	129	123	17,057	36,451	29,034	27,830	5,949	116,321	48,776	16,836	6,475	23,311	1,602	67,545	2,267	19·5
6 March	129	123	16,977	36,331	28,851	27,711	5,775	115,645	49,426	18,039	6,709	24,748	1,637	66,219	2,590	22·
13 „	130	123	16,589	35,897	28,554	27,405	5,628	114,073	49,664	17,586	8,175	25,761	1,580	64,409	2,734	24·
20 „	130	123	16,652	35,715	28,213	27,132	5,541	113,285	50,178	18,062	8,569	26,631	1,580	63,107	2,514	22·
27 „	130	123	16,575	35,293	27,698	26,700	5,294	111,560	50,747	17,102	9,160	26,262	1,547	60,813	2,248	20·
3 April	130	123	15,861	33,583	26,693	25,680	4,771	106,888	50,861	17,308	8,931	26,239	1,458	56,027	2,706	25·
10 „	130	124	15,740	33,068	26,073	25,037	4,537	104,455	50,531	17,476	8,657	26,133	1,452	53,924	2,613	25·

Appendix 6. This is a page from the Thirteenth Annual Report of the Poor Law Commissioners for Ireland. It show that the number of people in Irish workhouses on 4 April 1846 was 50,861, and a year later it had doubled to 106,88 The number of deaths on 4 April 1846 was 159 and on 3 April 1847 had increased to 2706.

Parliamentary Papers, Thirteenth Report of the Poor Law Commissioners 1847.

Image courtesy of the National Library of Ireland.

No. 11.

COMPARATIVE STATEMENT of the QUANTITIES of WHEAT and FLOUR, BARLEY and BARLEY-MEAL, OATS and OATMEAL exported from *Ireland* to *Great Britain* in the Years 1843, 1844, 1845, with those exported in the Eleven Months ending 5th December 1846.

	1843.	1844.	1845.	Average of Three Years.	*11 Months of 1846.	Increase.	Decrease.	Difference, Decrease.
	Qrs.	Qrs.	Qrs.	Qrs.	Qrs.	Qrs.	Qrs.	Qrs.
Wheat and Flour -	413,466	440,152	779,113	544,243	407,999	- -	136,244	
Barley and Barley Meal - - -	110,449	90,656	93,095	98,067	99,797	1,730	—	
								1,280,392
Oats and Oatmeal -	2,648,033	2,242,309	2,353,985	2,414,776	1,268,898	- -	1,145,878	
TOTALS - -	3,171,948	2,773,117	3,226,193	3,057,086	1,776,694	1,730	1,282,122	

* Account for Month ending 5 January 1847 not yet received.

Prepared from Accounts furnished by the Inspector-general of Imports and Exports.

Under 2 oz.

1.

Ordered, by The House of Commons, to be Printed,
19 January 1847.

(*Mr. Parker.*)

RETURNS relating to the IMPORT and EXPORT ENTRIES, PRICES, &c., of WHEAT and other GRAIN and FLOUR.

C O R N.

Appendix 7. This is a return to Parliament of the amount of grain which was exported from Ireland to England in 1843, 1844, 1845, and 1846. It showed that the average was 3,057,086 quarters of grain each year. It also showed that when the Corn Laws were repealed in June 1846, the amount exported from Ireland dropped by half. Cheap wheat was then brought into England from America. This would have put the Irish labourer out of work and would have led to hunger and starvation.

Parliamentary Papers, 1847 (1) *Corn Returns relating to the import and export entries, prices, &c., of wheat and other grain and flour*. Page image 10 of 10.

Image courtesy of the National Library of Ireland.

121

COUNTY	NAME of OWNER	Date of Sale	ORDNANCE VALUATION of each Lot by Townlands
Kerry		1850:	
Limerick			
Cork			
Galway	Charlotte Danelan	9 June	
Cork	Sir James Coter	4 June	See Observations
Galway	Thomas O'Brien, (J.D. Malley, Assignee of)	4 June	Ordnance Valuation of county Cork not completed
City of Dublin	George Davey	7 June	Fairfield
Kerry	Thomas C. Ponsonby	7 June	Ordnance Valuation of county Cork not completed
Clare	George Martyn	7 June	(Graggan (East)) (ditto (West)) (Penagh)
Limerick	A. O Rose	4 April & 3 June	Ordnance Valuation of county Limerick not completed
Cork	Chambre Corker	11 June	Ordnance Valuation of county Cork not completed
Londonderry	Jane Boyd	11 June	Longhanna, North and South
Tipperary	James Fitzpatrick	11 June	Ordnance Survey not completed of Tipperary
King's County	Richard Dancer	14 June	Derrinamuckley and Bawypark
City of Dublin	Robert Corballis	14 June	Ground-rents
Dublin	Robert Richardson	14 June	Not surveyed
Queen's County	Elizabeth Dought	14 June	
Roscommon	John M'Dermott	18 June	Tobernore
Waterford	G. B. Jackson		The Valuation of Waterford not completed

Appendix 8. This is a page from a Parliamentary return giving the names of all the landowners whose estates were seized in 1849-1853, through the Incumbered estates Act. Lord Russell passed an Act in 1849 making it very easy for any creditor to force a person off their land. Before this Act, only a bank or an institution holding a mortgage, could repossess an estate. After this act, any creditor could start proceedings to evict a landowner. This law was not passed for England, only for Ireland.

Parliamentary Papers, 1850 (615) Incumbered Estates (Ireland). *Return of all sales made under the authority of then Commissioners of Incumbered Estates, Ireland.*

Image courtesy of the National Library of Ireland.

BALLINROBE UNION

Dr. Dempster to the Commissioners:- November 30, 1847.

I have the honour to transmit copies of a return of the children and schools in this Union, and of my letter to Count Strzelecki, the agent of the British Relief Association, relating to the feeding and clothing of the children.

Enclosures

Ballinrobe Union,   Dr. James Dempster, Inspector.

Places	Children		Accommodation	Remarks
	Male	female	for	
Claremorris	60	40	180	
Muereen Claremorris	36	16		No return as to accommodation
Culliboe	27	11		Idem
Garristown		54	70	
Robeen				Industrial
Kilmaine	18	7	100	
Holly Mount	80	44	160	
Shrule	72	56	140	
Cong	25	27	..	school held in Roman Catholic Chapel
Cross Cong	30	27	80	
Balla Holly Mount	39	43	200	
Ballinrobe	40	15	60	Kept by Mr. Thomas Kenny, private teacher
Ballinrobe	40	6	90	Ditto Mr. Williams
Ballinrobe	21		60	Mr. Rooney, a classical teacher.
Carrowkeel Ross	104	101	206	Average of daily attendance varies, National
Ross Hill Ross	40	25	65	Lady Elizabeth Clements, patroness
Cloughbrack Ross	39	36	80	Private subscription
Finny Ross	26	20	60	Ditto
Ballindine	80	75	200	
Partry				Ample attendance
Ballybarron			600	by
Gortymore				feeding
Port Royal				the children
Tourmakeady, *alias* Cappaduff	28	46	200	
Castlekerke, *alias* Doon Rossa	60	87	300	An admirably conducted school under Captain and Mrs.Blake of Doon
Total	869	741	2851	James Dempster, M.D.

This table shows that Dr. Dempster, the Inspector of the Poor Law Union for Ballinrobe, gave the number of children attending school in that Union as 869 males and 741 females, that is 1610. It is from a report on relief of distress. Count Strzeletski gave it as 11,510. 1847-48 (919) (955) (999) *Papers relating to proceedings for relief of distress, and state of unions and workhouses in Ireland, 1848* Page image 391 of 2047.

Enclosure 2. Table showing the details connected with the Relief to Children since November, 1847, up to the week ending 30th April 1848:-

Unions	The Denomination of Schools				Total No. of children Receiving Relief	Total No. of Rations issued since 30th Nov 1847, to 30th April, 1848
	National	Established Church	Dissenter	Catholic		
Ballina	3,767	1,660	2,097	8,256	15,780	1,882,188
Belmullet	1,747	661	-------	1,780	4,188	498,535
Ballinrobe	2,802	708	-------	8,000	11,510	835,499
Ballyshannon	4,582	864	62	4,327	9,835	998,962
Bantry	2,258	1,168	------	6,954	10,380	1,227,282
Boyle	2,810	1,030	140	815	4,795	398,415
Cahirciveen	2,940	450	------	------	3,390	489,440
Carrick- On- Shannon	2,140	1,330	70	1,290	4,830	635,152
Castlebar	1,115	444	78	3,598	5,235	640,514
Castlerea	2,649	1,429	------	6,951	11.029	1,061,907
Clifden	516	1,174	440	2,568	4,698	527,723
Donegal	1,364	2,813	610	848	5,635	504,399
Galway	3,547	278	250	2,736	6,811	857,563
Glenties	5,843	1,218	136	------	7,197	616,021
Kenmare	1,260	356	------	3,110	4,726	508,186
Kilrush	3,362	319	------	------	3,681	426,503
Listowel	5,620	178	------	2,331	8,129	622,517
Manor- Hamilton	1,100	66	------	780	1,946	97,622
Milford	1,746	964	324	------	3,034	321,965
Mohill	326	200	------	------	526	93,695
Roscommon	998	571	------	------	1,569	136,444
Skibbereen	10,597	3,102	50	7,801	21,640	3,129,091
Sligo	5,192	4,080	420	5,280	14,972	1,695,554
Swineford	6,030	------	------	15,679	21,709	1,857,030
Tralee	2,586	1,143	------	1.196	4,925	565,838
Tuam	526	46	------	435	1,007	80,549
Westport,	2,650	736	44	4,820	8,250	1,021,377
	80,073	26,988	4,721	89,645	201,427	21,621,881

This report prepared by Count Strzeletski and printed in the Annual Report of the Poor Law Commissioners for 1848 shows that he states that the number of children attending school in the Ballinrobe Union is 11,510.

1847-48 (963), *First annual report of the Commissioners for Administering the Laws for Relief of the Poor in Ireland, with appendices.* Page image 128 of 197.

We select the following as some of the more extensive cases of eviction as given in this return :—In the union of Armagh, 30 persons evicted at the suit of W. M'Geough Bond, Esq. In the union of Ballina, (Mayo), eighty-five were evicted by the under agent to the Earl of Arran ; 27 by the agent of Colonel Knox Gore, and 116 by the agent to Sir W. H. Palmer, Bart. In the union of Ballinasloe (Galway), 110 persons by the agent to the Rev. E. Paget, J. Lyons, Esq., &c. In the union of Ballinrobe (Mayo), 37 by the bailiff to Lord Oranmore ; 43 by the bailiff to R. D. Browne, Esq., M.P., 35 by the bailiff to Lord Kilmaine ; and 51 by the bailiff of Colonel Knox. In the union of Ballymena (county Antrim), 40 by the agent to Lord O'Neill. In the union of Ballyshannon (Donegal), 40 by the agent of Col. Conolly. In the union of Banbridge (county Down), 26 by the agent to the Marquis of Downshire ; 43 by the agent to Count de Salis. In the union of Boyle (Roscommon), &c., 45 by the agent of Lord Lorton ; and 86 at the suit of the agent of Lord De Freyne ; and 91 by an agent under the Court of Chancery. In the union of Carlow, 65 by the agent of the Earl of Bessborough. In the union of Carrick-on-Suir (Leitrim), 35 by the agent of R. O. Gore, Esq., M.P., 23 by the agent of Lord V. Southwood ; and 32 by the agent of T. J. Barton, Esq. In the union of Castlebar, 31 by the agent of the Earl of Lucan, and 68 by the agent of Sir R. Palmer. In the union of Castleblaney (Armagh), 55 by J. M'Watty, Esq., for Walter M'Geough Bond, Esq., and 21 by the same gentleman for T. P.

Appendix 9. This is part of a report in the Anglo Celt giving names of some of the Landlords who had evicted their tenants in 1849. The list included the names of the Lord Lieutenant, the Earl of Bessborough, of many Lords and members of Parliament, such as Lord Farnham and the Earl of Lucan, and of many English Lords who were absentee landlords. The Anglo Celt Friday October 19 1849

RATES ON CAVAN UNION.

Return of the amount of each rate struck on the several electoral divisions of the Cavan union:—

Arvagh.

Rate	Date	Year	s.	d.
First rate,	14th June,	1842	0	5
Second rate,	21st February,	1843	0	7½
Third rate,	13th February,	1844	0	2½
Fourth rate,	22nd April,	1845	0	2½
Fifth rate,	20th January,	1846	0	5
Sixth rate,	19th January,	1847	0	2½
Seventh rate,	11th December,	1847	3	0
Eighth rate,	11th July,	1848	4	0
Ninth rate,	6th April,	1849	2	6

Ballintample.

Rate	Date	Year	s.	d.
First rate,	14th June,	1842	0	5
Second rate,	21st February,	1843	0	7½
Third rate,	13th February,	1844	0	2½
Fourth rate,	22nd April,	1845	0	2½
Fifth rate,	20th January,	1846	0	5
Sixth rate,	19th January,	1847	0	2½
Seventh rate,	11th December,	1847	3	0
Eighth rate,	11th July,	1848	3	0
Ninth rate,	6th April,	1849	2	6

Ballyconnell.

Rate	Date	Year	s.	d.
First rate,	14th June,	1842	0	5
Second rate,	21st February,	1843	0	7½
Third rate,	13th February,	1844	0	5
Fourth rate,	22nd April,	1845	0	7½
Fifth rate,	20th January,	1846	1	0½
Sixth rate,	19th January,	1847	0	2½
Seventh rate,	11th December,	1847	2	2
Eighth rate,	11th July,	1848	3	0
Ninth rate,	6th April,	1849	1	8

Ballyhaise.

Rate	Date	Year	s.	d.
First rate,	14th June,	1842	0	5
Second rate,	21st February,	1843	0	7½
Third rate,	13th February,	1844	0	7½
Fourth rate,	22nd April,	1845	0	10
Fifth rate,	20th January,	1846	1	3
Sixth rate,	19th January,	1847	1	8
Seventh rate,	11th December,	1847	3	0
Eighth rate,	11th July,	1848	5	0
Ninth rate,	6th April,	1849	2	6

Ballymachugh.

Rate	Date	Year	s.	d.
First rate,	14th June,	1842	5	0
Second rate,	21st February,	1843	0	7½
Third rate,	13th February,	1844	0	2½
Fourth rate,	22nd April,	1845	0	0
Fifth rate,	20th January,	1846	0	5
Sixth rate,	19th January,	1847	0	0
Seventh rate,	11th December,	1847	3	0
Eighth rate,	11th July,	1848	3	0
Ninth rate,	6th April,	1849	2	6

Belturbet.

Rate	Date	Year	s.	d.
First rate,	14th June,	1842	0	5
Second rate,	21st February,	1843	0	7½
Third rate,	13th February,	1844	0	5
Fourth rate,	22nd April,	1845	0	5
Fifth rate,	20th January,	1846	1	3
Sixth rate,	19th January,	1847	2	6
Seventh rate,	11th December,	1847	3	0
Eighth rate,	11th July,	1848	5	0
Ninth rate,	6th April,	1849	3	4

Butlersbridge.

Rate	Date	Year	s.	d.
First rate,	14th June,	1842	0	5
Second rate,	21st February,	1843	0	7½
Third rate,	13th February,	1844	0	5
Fourth rate,	22nd April,	1845	0	5
Fifth rate,	20th January,	1846	0	10
Sixth rate,	19th January,	1847	1	3
Seventh rate,	11th December,	1847	3	3
Eighth rate,	11th July,	1848	4	0
Ninth rate,	6th April,	1849	2	6

Cavan.

Rate	Date	Year	s.	d.
First rate,	14th June,	1842	0	5
Second rate,	21st February,	1843	0	7½
Third rate,	13th February,	1844	0	10
Fourth rate,	22nd April,	1845	0	10
Fifth rate,	20th January,	1846	1	3
Sixth rate,	19th January,	1847	1	5½
Seventh rate,	11th December,	1847	3	0
Eighth rate,	11th July,	1848	3	0
Ninth rate,	6th April,	1849	2	6

Anglo Celt Cavan Friday April 13 1849.

This article shows the increase in taxes under the Poor Laws, from the striking of the first rate in 1842 to the ninth rate in 1849, in the Cavan Union.

The first rate was 5 pence in the pound or about 2% of the annual rental value of the land. (there were 240 pence in £1.)

In 1847, when the Relief Works of Lord Russell, and of the Chief Secretary for Ireland, Henri Labouchere, were introduced, there were two rates for that year. One was for about 2.5 pence, in January 1847, but the second was for about 3 shillings, or 15%. (3 shillings was 36 pence. There were 12 pennies in a shilling). This was an increase of 7 times the first rate, in a period of five years.

Bibliography

The most important sources for this book were the records of debates held in the House of Commons and the House of Lords, during the period from 1836 to 1854. These can be accessed on the internet at the website of the House of Parliament in London. That is at https://api.parliament.uk/historic-hansard/sittings/1800s

The second most important source was the collection of Parliamentary records which have been digitized by the University of Southampton and which are available online at www.dippam.ac.uk. This resource covers "Documenting Ireland, Parliament, People and Migration, and Enhanced British Parliamentary Papers on Ireland. https://quod.lib.umich.edu/j/jahc/3310410.0007.302/--eppi-enhanced-british-parliamentary-papers-in-ireland-1801.

Other relevant books are:-

Butt, Isaac. *A voice for Ireland. The Famine in the land.* What has been done and what is to be done. The Dublin University magazine. Dublin 1847.

Butt, Isaac. *A letter to Lord Morpeth.* The Poor-law Bill for Ireland examined; its provisions and the Report of Mr.Nicholls contrasted with the facts proved by the Poor law Inquiry Commission. Dublin, 1837.

Crowley, John; Smith, William J.; Murphy, Mike. *Atlas of the Great Irish Famine.* Cork, 2012.

Coogan, Tim Pat. *The Famine Plot.* New York, 2012.

Disraeli, Benjamin. *Lord George Bentinck; a political biography.* London 1852.

Edwards, Robin Dudley; and Williams, T.D. eds. The Great Famine. Dublin, 1956.

Frazer, Sir William. *Hic et Ubique.* London 1893.

Griffith, Richard. *Outline of the Geology of Ireland.* London, 1838.

Kennedy, John Pitt. *Instruct; Employ; Don't Hang Them;* or Ireland tranquilized without soldiers and Enriched without English Capital. London, 1835.

Kinealy, Christine. *This Great Calamity: The Irish Famine 1845-1852.* Boulder, 1995.

Malthus, Thomas. *An Essay on the Principle of Population, or a view of its Past and Present Effects on Human Happiness.* London 1807.

Marx, Karl, and Engels, Frederick. R. Dixon ed. *Ireland and the Irish Question.* Moscow 1971.

Mitchell, John. *The Last Conquest of Ireland (perhaps).* Dublin, 1861.

Nicholls, George. *Poor Laws-Ireland. Three reports to Her Majesty's principal Secretary of State for the Home Department.* London: HMSO, 1838.

O'Grada, Cormac. *The Great Irish Famine.* Dublin 1989.

Porteir, C. Ed. *The Great Irish Famine.* Dublin 1995.

Poulet Scrope, George. *Some notes of a tour in England, Scotland and Ireland, made with a view to the inquiry, whether our labouring population be really redundant.* London, 1849.

Sen, Amartya. *Poverty and Famines, an Essay on Entitlements and Deprivation.* Oxford. 1961.

Trevelyan, Charles. *The Irish Crisis.* London, 1848.

Wilkinson, George. *Practical Geology and Ancient Architecture of Ireland.* London and Dublin, 1845.

Woodham Smith, Cecil. *The great hunger: Ireland 1845-1849.* New York 1962.

The Discovery of the Potato Blight in Ireland Daniel MacDonald (1821-1853).
(Irish Folklore Commission U.C.D.)

The face of the central figure is very similar to the face of Sir Robert Peel, which can be seen in portraits of him on the website of the National Portrait Gallery in London. He is rising above a sheaf of corn or wheat. Underneath the grain are rotting potatoes. The artist is linking the plight of the Irish to the actions of Peel in repealing the Corn Laws. The face of the figure kneeling on the right is similar to portraits of John Mitchel, the writer and member of the Young Irelanders. The artist is echoing the accusations of John Mitchel that "The Almighty sent the potato blight but the English caused the famine".

The illustration is reproduced with kind permission of the Irish Folklore Commission, University College Dublin.

Acknowledgements

The inspiration for this book came from exploring the ruins of the workhouse in our local village of Bawnboy. Just a few miles from the border with the North of Ireland, this workhouse was a refuge for people north and south of the border for seventy years, until 1922, when it was closed down.

It has taken me seven years to research the origins of the workhouses, and the Poor Laws, which provided for these buildings to be erected. In this research I have been helped enormously by the staff of many public institutions. The staff in Ballinamore library, in Co. Leitrim, have been very supportive. In particular I would like to thank Mary Conefey, who has pointed me to many useful sources. The staff of the Johnston Library in Cavan, helped by giving me access to handwritten minute books of the Bawnboy Workhouse. They also hold copies of the Anglo Celt, which has vivid accounts of the famine times. Thanks are due to the Anglo Celt for these records.

I am indebted to the staff of the National Library, in Dublin, who have been very helpful in allowing me access to the original records of the debates in the Houses of Parliament during the famine period. In particular Glen Dunne has been understanding of my need to reproduce digital images of material from Parliamentary Papers during the famine times. I am very grateful for his help.

The staff in the Irish Architectural Archives assisted me to study the plans for the Irish workhouses which were drawn up by George Wilkinson between 1839 and 1852. Criostcir Mac Carthaigh of the Irish Folklore Commission let me view the records of stories about the famine in the Cavan Area, which were collected in 1945, 100 years after the famine. In addition, he has kindly given me permission to reproduce the painting by Daniel MacDonald of "The Discovery of the Potato Blight in Ireland", which is held in the Folklore Commission and which was given to University College Dublin by Cecil Woodham Smith.

I am also wish to acknowledge the assistance of the staff of the National Archives of Ireland, the staff in the Public Record Office in Kew, and the staff in the Public Record Office of Northern Ireland.

I tried hard to find a portrait of Edward Twisleton, who was the chief Commissioner for the administration of the Poor Laws in Ireland from 1845 to 1849, during the worst years of the famine. I finally wrote to the place where he was buried, in Oxfordshire in England. I was delighted to receive back immediately a copy of a portrait, from the Hon. Martin Fiennes, with permission to use it in this book. I appreciate this kindness.

I wish to express my thanks to my family. I am particularly indebted to my son Killian, who has stayed with me every step of the way, and who has helped me enormously with the format of the book and with his practical IT skills.

Finally I wish to express my gratitude to Jan for the kindness and patience with which he has supported me through my many endeavours. It has made a great difference to the way in which I could concentrate on this project. Bedankt honey.

Index